LOS ANGELES'S

BEST DIVE BARS

LOS ANGELES'S
BEST DIVE BARS

Drinking and Diving in the City of Angels

LINA LECARO

Brooklyn, New York

Printed in the USA
10 9 8 7 6 5 4 3 2 1

Gamble Guides is an imprint of
Ig Publishing
392 Clinton Avenue
Brooklyn, NY 11238
www.igpub.com

ACKNOWLEDGEMENTS

To my husband Albert for his un-dying support (including watching the li'l one while his wife went drinking and dallying about Los Angeles) and joining me on the shadier treks. To my mom and dad, John and Sandra, for their good genetics, which surely supplied me with both the energy to go out and wherewithal to consume so much alcohol, and (hopefully) not look like it. To my drinking buddies: Heidi, Wendy, Leslie, and Sylvia for their fearless accompaniment and astute observations. And to my daughter, Charlotte Elsie Cadillac Pinkerson ("Cadillac" is in homage to Cadillac margaritas!), who taught me patience and moderation, which I needed while "researching" this book. Would have had a lot more hungover mornings if I didn't practice both. And it's no fun to write with a hangover. Trust me, I know.

Los Angeles's Best Dive Bars
(arranged by location)

San Fernando Valley
(Van Nuys, Sherman Oaks, Studio City, North Hollywood)
Liquid Zoo
Pogo's
Chimneysweep Lounge
Fox Fire Room
Maeve's Residuals
Starlite Room
Tonga Hut

Burbank
The Blue Room
Sardo's
Tin Horn Flats

Glendale
Big Fish
Corner Bar
Dave's
Winchester Room
Tony's Bar
Tops Club

Sunland & La Crescenta
The Sundown
Where else, Inc?
Whisperz
Up Th' Hill

Pasadena
The 35er
Colorado Bar
R Place

East LA/San Gabriel Valley
Whittier, Rosemead, Highland Park, Boyle Heights
Embers Lounge
Poor Denny's Saloon
Spike's
Footsies
Johnny's
Little Cave
Eastside Luv

*Downtown & Downtown Adjacent
Little Tokyo, Chinatown, Civic Center, Angelino Heights, West Lake
Far Bar
Grand Star
Hop Louie
Back Door Pub
Bar 107
Five Stars Bar
Hank's
King Eddy Saloon
La Cita Bar
Redwood Bar
Tony's Saloon
M House
Silver Platter

Echo Park
Gold Room
Little Joy
The Short Stop

Silver Lake/Atwater
Akbar
Le Barcito
The Eagle
Hyperion Tavern
The Red Lion
Silver Lake Lounge
Smog Cutter
Tee Gee
Tiki Ti

Los Feliz
Bigfoot Lodge
The Dresden
The Drawing Room
The Roost
Ye Rustic Inn

Koreatown and Miracle Mile
Frank N Hanks
HMS Bounty
Little Bar
One Eye Jacks

Hollywood
The Bar
The Burgundy Room
Crane's Hollywood Tavern
Frolic Room
Gold Diggers
Jumbo's Clown Room
Lotus Lounge
Powerhouse
Prime Time
Relax
Three Clubs
The Spotlight

Vine Bar
White Horse

West Hollywood & Sunset Strip
Barney's Beanery (bar area)
The Cat Club
(Over) The Rainbow
Ye Coach & Horses

Fairfax District
Kibitz Room

Culver City
Backstage Bar & Grill
The Cinema Bar
Cozy Inn
Joxer's Daly
Scarlet Lady Saloon
Tattle Tale

Mar Vista
Lost & Found

Santa Monica
Chez Jay
The Daily Pint
Gaslite
The Joker
Speakeasy

Inglewood, Mid-City
The Annex
The Beacon
The Cork

"An intellectual says a simple thing in a hard way. An artist says a hard thing in a simple way." –Charles Bukowski

Introduction

No city in the entire globe comes with pre-conceived notions about its nightlife in quite the way that Los Angeles does. Celebutards, tempestuous traffic, voracious valets, swarming stalkerazzi, three figure bottle service tables, vamp-packed velvet ropes, gorilla-ish gatekeepers, rockstar DJs (and their famous girlfriends), and tome-like guestlists can make for an annoying after dark audaciousness.

Unfortunately, for many who don't live here this is all they know of LA. All the clubbin' clichés are here, yes, but despite what TMZ or *The Hills* or *Entourage* like to glorify, there is so much more beneath and beyond Tinseltown's after dark façade. LA is a multi-cultural Mecca, easily one of the most-spread out cities in the country, and a hub of creativity unlike anywhere else in the world. Despite our penchant for shopping malls, condos and face lifts (structural or otherwise), much history and character remains here. Those who've lived here all their lives know it. Those who've come here to be inspired by it—as opposed to simply "make it"—know it too.

Prolific writers like Charles Bukowski and Raymond Chandler also knew it. As Bukowski in particular understood only too well, nowhere is this gritty essence more apparent than inside the older, quirkier places where we imbibe. Inspired revelry can blossom in swanky locales, sure, but more often than not, it's the unfettered, even grimy grottos that amuse and arouse... and allow for real human connections. As a born and bred Angeleno, and music and nightlife journalist who has made intrepid after-dark delving my life for over twenty years now, I've gone back and forth between devotion and detestation for my hometown's overly-conspicuous havens of consumption, but my love for authentic, wearied watering holes—aka dives—has never wavered.

A night of frou-frou cocktails, fanciful frocks, and crowd-pleaser DJs spinning mash-ups of Journey and 50 Cent for alpha-babes (A, B, and C listers) can be a cheesy romp—especially if said 'tails are strong—but ultimately, the evenings that have stayed with me long after the next day (and sometimes day after that) hangovers have taken place at neighborhood hovels, loud rawkin' joints and unfettered dive bars filled with familiar tunes and familiar faces. My first legal guzzles took place in such a spot (a long-gone Silver Lake tavern called The Shamrock on Sunset, later to become a strip club called Cheetahs). Actually, I had a (bad) fake ID then, so I guess it wasn't so legal, and come to think of it, I got in a couple times without the thing. But then, that was a dive for ya.

Which brings us to the highly debatable question of what constitutes a "dive." One need only surf through the internet or strike up a chat at a house party to hear some very contentious opinions... and everybody seems to have one. But there is no formula for determining a bar's diviness and it can't be simplified like some Jeff Foxworthy-type comedy skit ("If someone asks to see your ID and you show 'em your belt-buckle, you might be a redneck... or at a dive bar.") A bar's diviness must be considered in context of many different things, things that go even beyond the neighborhood, the regulars, and the décor. "You can put lipstick on a pig, but it's still a pig," one of my fellow guzzler gals blurted out during a discussion about the revamped dive bar trend. While some dives are able to maintain their swine-y swagger even after going through a remodeling, many sadly do not. It kind of depends on how much of an oinker that place was to begin with and what kind of "lipstick" it is being applied—and who is doing the applying. What I'm getting at here is that a dive doesn't necessarily have to be a dump or a sty. It doesn't *have* to have cheap drinks, but it usually does. It doesn't *have* to be old, but it usually is. It's an alchemic blend of these elements and more that conjure the almost mystical meld of menace and merriment that makes a dive a dive.

Before I go further, a word needs to be said about the dreaded "hipster" dive. If I said that every bar in this book had to be hipster-free, you'd be reading a pamphlet right now. By definition—and this has been true for at least the past couple of decades—"hip" people are those who, for the most part, pooh-pooh the pretentiousness of slick, pricey rooms, especially in LA, where these are so prevalent. These "hipsters" want to be the first to discover a new (or rather old) dive, even if they don't want to be the only "cool" person there. It goes something like this: trendy type discovers dive and invites friends to the hush-hush hub. The crew revels in its unknown community cave and pats itself on the back for the business it's brought to the formerly dreary space. Then, *wah-wah-waaah*... the word gets out. Inevitably, more stylishly-tressed types start popping in and the local color starts to get muted by tats and snazzy retro hats. Soon, the original dive dwellers who discovered the place move on, in search of the next secret shack to attack. And the cycle continues. Dives heat up and cool down like this all time, but in a nutshell, whether they're packed with trendoids or toothless old-timers, infiltrated by a small group or (more common lately) a club promoter bringing in hundreds of guests, dives in LA are vulnerable to hipster invasion, precisely because they are run-down, real and, yes, *un-hip*. Sure, there's a bunch that have yet to be invaded (and the best are included here), but sorry to break it to you, it may only be a matter of time for most of 'em, especially once this book makes the—cough, cough—best seller lists. I, for one don't have a problem with it. The best atmosphere—dive bar or not—is all about the mish-mash, the kooky disparities, and the obvious and not so obvious differences that make us human.

It is my hope that this guide will serve as a boozy bible for natives like myself (who've maybe driven by a grimy spot with its seductive old "cocktails" sign and unscrupulous and or just interesting characters outside and pondered what might be inside) as well as visitors to LA looking for drinking dens boasting this mystifying mix of humanity, history, lethal drinks and possibly lethal atmosphere. For this reason, I've tried to include a pretty diverse cross-section. Some have food, some offer entertainment, some have great selection, some not so much. Finally, some are somewhat tourist friendly while some are totally convict friendly, so distinguished by dive ratings at the end of each write-up: 5 beer bottles being the diviest, 1 being the least divey.

DIVE O METER

All bars are rated on a scale of one to five bottles of beer, with five bottles denoting the diviest.

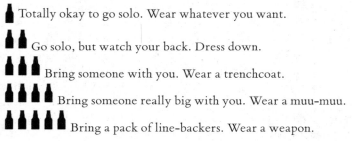

Totally okay to go solo. Wear whatever you want.

Go solo, but watch your back. Dress down.

Bring someone with you. Wear a trenchcoat.

Bring someone really big with you. Wear a muu-muu.

Bring a pack of line-backers. Wear a weapon.

Hardcore divers (and there are many) will no doubt take issue with some of the bars that made the cut here, but if I felt the place had something special to offer and I could check off at least half the criteria from my list below, I included it. If you gotta problem with that buster, let's take it outside next time I see ya at one of 'em, okay?

1. The decrepit winos, non-English speaking regulars, and semi-homeless hell-raisers hold on and even comingle with the new slew of pretty party peeps that've discovered the place.
2. The bar prices have stayed (relatively) the same after many moons and goons.
3. It's been around forever and even when attempts at remodeling, revamping, repainting or re-anything happen, grungy ghosts remain. Also, it doesn't stay pristine for long.
4. No Crystal or Dom or fine wines or imports (unless you count some vile Mexican moonshine the owner brought in for special occasions).
5. The Stepford starlet known as Paris Hilton has never—and will never—step a hot pink mani'd toe inside.

6. The bathrooms make ya wanna heave-ho and have seen lots of heaving and ho-ing in the past.
7. An old school feel that often includes old-school eats, old-school smells and old-school conversation (because of, you know, all the old people).
8. Upon arrival you suddenly want some charcoal and a pad, 'cause it's real sketchy!

Or….

9. The neighborhood ain't necessarily that bad, but the people who get comfortably numb there night after night all live nearby—and if you're an outsider, they'd like you to (un)kindly stay out!
10. The Crack factor:

    -As seen in ceilings and seating (and big behinds atop the bar-stools).

    -As in powdered noses/aluminum foil pipes.

    -As in the sound heard during a drunken brawl.

Pogo's

SAN FERNANDO VALLEY

VAN NUYS
SHERMAN OAKS
STUDIO CITY
NORTH HOLLYWOOD

Liquid Zoo

7214 Sepulveda Blvd
Phone: (818) 997-3818

Though there's been somewhat of a long-standing hostility between those who live in LA proper and those who reside in the area known as the San Fernando Valley, aka "the 818" (remember Alicia Silverstone's hesitation to attend a "Valley Party" in *Clueless*), this has definitely changed over the past several years. With affordable housing becoming less available in area codes like 213, 323 and especially 310, many have migrated to the area known for its higher temps and (in some snobbier opinions) trashier inhabitants. Of course, the assumptions and stereotypes about the region (perpetuated by the "ohmigod" embued slang of Frank Zappa's "Valley Girl" and the film of same name in the 1980s) are as close-minded and oversimplified as those about Los Angeles itself. Both are equally diverse with sketchy parts and ritzy parts, wholesome and not so wholesome goings-on.

The Van Nuys watering hole aptly named Liquid Zoo definitely belongs in the latter category. No trendy Galleria girls here, unless you count a couple of Rubenesque lasses in ill-fitting Forever 21 mini skirts or the punky bartender showing off her chest tattoo in a low-cut leopard number (It is a zoo after all). To be fair, L.Z. might not be the Valley's classiest destination, but it's not as creepy as it once was. Though it used to be a hotspot for hookers and pushers, the crowds these days are mostly harmless drunks or hopeless dreamers honing their "craft" during the bar's open mic nights (mostly comedy and singer-songwriter showcases). I visited the Zoo on a Tuesday night and was treated to a guy whose guitar strumming was only meeker than his falsetto. Nobody in the bar seemed to notice him or even look his way. "Dive Bar Divas," a Sunday night showcase features more real raw talents, or so a ponytail-sporting man is overheard boasting. With lots of tables and chairs, plus the tiny corner stage across from the counter and pool table crammed in by the exit, this small-mirrored box is almost claustrophobic, especially when the live music starts. Unless you're there to support a pal up there crooning, hit the Zoo before the amps get set up. In addition to discount-priced drinkees, they often put out free food (Fetticini Alfredo is a specialty). Early arrival is also suggested to assure there'll be something left to grub before the Zoo's more ravenous regulars let loose.

Pogo's

17314 Saticoy St.
Phone: (818) 705-9396

Dive Bar Rating

Like Liquid Zoo, Pogo's is in one of the Valley's less than charming areas, but unlike the Zoo, which has transformed itself—somewhat—into a music destination, the sole purpose of entering Pogo's is to get completely and utterly shit-faced stupid.

The crowd is rough and full of revelry. Hoods (as in Eminem lookalikes in head-shrouding hoodies) almost come to blows over a dart game only to knuckle-bump minutes later in one corner, while sloshed shrieks of victory from a group of loud and loose Latin ladies in velour tracksuits ring out near the pool table. All the while, cock rock blasts from the juke. The busty barmaid—sporting a spat of tats not unlike the lass behind Liquid's counter—does her best to make sure all are satiated with very strong, very cheap drinks (five smacker range). The criminal-looking clusters might be more about the nearby tattoo shop than the actual rap sheet quota of patrons here, but either way, there's an air of danger and dare I say it, excitement that seems to energize the room around midnight or so.

As for the look of place, it's your standard faux wood, red tables and chairs, neon lit spot (the Tim McGraw light is priceless) with a very *My Name Is Earl*-ish ambience, i.e. lots of bandannas, trucker caps and cowboy hats. The bathroom, like many dive bar ladies laboratories, is perplexing. For some reason, there's always a separate but useless holding area before the actual toilet in places like this. Whether they're clean or repulsive, replete with mirrors, basins or nothing at all, these closet-sized spaces are always too small and definitely not where most gals might want to primp or um, powder their noses. (They irritate almost as much as the ubiquitous urine trickled toilet seats). Ladies, if you're gonna squat, do it right and really exercise those thigh muscles. Aim, and not half-assed either, please, as Pogo's is particularly peculiar and prone to pee-drops since the light above the john doesn't seem to work. You'll need to keep the door cracked to see your business, which means the bee-yotch behind you can too. Of course, most of the women here are too wasted to care.

Chimneysweep Lounge

4354 Woodman Ave.
Phone: (818) 783-3348

Dive Bar Rating

With a name like Chimneysweep, one might assume a sullied old shaft, but this bar is surprisingly well kept for a place that opened in 1962. Tucked inside a mundane mini-mall next to a Thai food joint, and just a skip away from the busy, consumer-minded stretch that is Ventura Blvd, Chimney provides a quaint if alcohol-amped atmosphere, an escape from the sleek retail havens that surround it.

Cartoony drawings of dusty faced little Oliver Twist-ish fellows (chimney sweeps, before those pesky child labor laws) adorn the walls, giving the place a whimsical feel. However, the par de resistance is definitely the shagadelic sixties ski lodge-style fireplace in the center of the room, a big black cone-shaped gas powered thing encircled by a stone-specked table, perfect for placing drinks—or the free popcorn baskets—on while you get toasty. Actually, make that roasty, as the fireplace kicks butt and even a perpetually chilly filly like moi was sweatin' it after sitting near it for a half hour or so.

The place itself may not be very big (there is an adjacent game room with pool, video games and darts), but each corner provides a unique experience. Sitting at the bar, for example, is entirely different from lounging in the red booth-lined crevices and the fireplace area. As is the case at most old bars, the stools are where "the usuals" sit, as in "I'll have the usual." While there's something comforting about the ritual of popping atop the same stool day after day, catching up with one's BFF (bartender friend forever), the 'Sweep is not that kind of bar. Rick, the uber-serious server usually behind the counter, ain't a big talker, you see. He even printed out the beer list and posted it on the wall so that he can simply point when asked about the selection. Make your choice quick or else you'll be on the receiving end of quite an irritated look.

LOS ANGELES'S BEST DIVE BARS

Fox Fire Room

12516 Magnolia Blvd
Phone: (818) 766-1344

Deciding what to have at this gregarious Valley scrap always seems to be easier when you sit on a bar stool.. and you're female. A friendly gentlemen will be sitting there too, usually alone, and he'll likely tell you what's good, what's cheap and what's smart, peppering the forced conversation with adages like, "liquor then beer, never fear... beer than liquor never sicker" and "life is too short.. to drink cheap liquor." Okay, the second one doesn't really apply at Foxfire, which gives some of the best buzz for your buck in the city.

Vodka crans are all the way live for five (bucks), Bloody Mary's will bludgeon your organs and sizzle your tongue for a couple clams more, and shots are filled to the brim every single time. The Fox, as the regulars call it, has been in biz since the seventies and it's got an un-touched, old-fashioned feel thanks to items big and small: those witty little cartoon-covered cocktail napkins, visible security cameras, flirty Sam Malone-alike bartenders (if you're a wimpy shooter like me, the Friday guy will cheer you on while you try to act tough and down your poison in one gulp), and funny fixtures like ball lamps with faces drawn on 'em. The room's scheme also has all the requisites: red booths and bar chairs, cheap wood everywhere, and a birthday board. (The years of birth may not be posted up on the board, but most regulars have been guzzling for half a century or more, easy).

The Fox doesn't get too many hip hordes, but the crowds did get younger after Paul Thomas Anderson used the room as a backdrop for the film Magnolia (the street where Foxy calls home). Since then, you might see a few more shaggy heads, ironic tees, and man ponytails (in homage to Tom Cruise?) in the mix, especially when karaoke (c)rocks up the room on Sundays. Cruise crazies aside, there is no better song to sing here than Bob Segar's "Old Time Rock n' Roll." After all, newer Valley bars, like today's music, ain't got the same soul.

Maeve's Residuals

11042 Ventura Blvd.
Phone: (818) 761-8301

Dive Bar Rating

🍾🍾

Upon my first visit to Maeve's, I was surprised by the multitude of motley crews who frequented the mini-mall den, and I *am* referencing the band that Tommy Lee slaps skins with. The actor types (the moniker references the joint's long-standing policy of comping its patrons a drink if they show their near worthless residual check stubs for a buck or under) are here too, sure, but amid the "character faces" or "struggling starlets" there's a decidedly more hardcore-looking smatter of regulars; we're talking stretched earlobes and face tattoos. The average Joes, sports buffs (Maeve's even has its own softball team) and yes, would-be thespians, are more chatty/less clique-y than the black-haired leather lovers, but by the bewitching hour, modest Maeve's acquires a heightened house party feel, and the liquid courage quotient sees everyone gabbing and guzzling as one.

Part of this homey quality comes from the look of the place, which features a living room area with old couches and plants on one side, a long bar in the center of the room, and an elevated brick platform facing it. Upon the platform, a row of movie theatre style chairs sit in front of a mural that says "RESIDUALS" in the famed Hollywood sign letters. There's some tables and additional wicker chairs scattered about up there too, some with holes so big that small bums could easily fall through (They call it lived in). The place really wants to be its patrons home away from home too... there's a pile of game controllers (used for the Buzztime Trivia play-a-long TV games), earmarked old paperbacks, and WiFi! Maeve's also gives out free hot dogs, chili and popcorn during all televised sporting events, which are broadcast on six TV screens.

The tap selection is nice and fairly priced, there's a couple dart boards with real darts not those annoying electronic things, and the internet jukebox always seems to be playing something classic: Steely Dan, The Eagles, Steve Miller. Karaoke on Sundays packs the house, and it's here that you'll see and hear the "discover me" hungry denizens the place is known for. Ample parking is available in the mini-mall (which is often as much of scene as inside the bar, since it's where the colorful smokers/tokers gather), but if you're thinking of hopping over to the Fox & Hounds (Maeve's snazzier pubby competition across the street), don't, unless you're down for a dogfight. It's enemy territory and you will be towed.

Free, yes, FREE(!) Food

White Horse (cookies, hot dogs)

Liquid Zoo (pasta some nights)

Gold Room (tacos)

Maeve's Residuals (hot dogs game nights)

Tops Club (Menudo Tuesdays)

Free popcorn at Gaslite, Hank's, The Roost, 35er, Backdoor Pub, Chimneysweep

Starlite Room

11411 Moorpark St
Phone: (818) 766-5807

Dive Bar Rating

I'm sure I'll get no arguments from either the locals, the staff, or occasional visitors from other parts of town about the Starlite's dive status. From its swingy saloon doors to its stone-covered fireplace (like something out of the *Brady Bunch* house) and wood-paneled interior to its stiff drinks and loud, loose crowd, this is a dive. And at the Starlite, "dive" is not a slight in the least. The tenders are friendly (sometimes newbies even get a freebie), the sauce selections reasonably priced (4-5 bills, cash only, for basic mixed cocktails) and the room is laid out for maximum interaction, the pool table being the central point near the middle of often clamorous customer carousing. Ladies and gents walking past it to get to the loo have a good chance of getting poked with a cue if they're not looking… and good looking.

A warning to women: the bathroom has the worst lighting of any bar in this book. Don't get depressed. If you're drunk it's even worse, so forgo the mirror altogether if you can. Primping is in fact, unnecessary here. In fact, if you're too made up, you'll probably get some catty looks from the other ladies in the house, especially the older ones in sweats. The Starlite is not a pickup joint by any means, but hooking up can and does happen with a well-sauced stew this sundry. Females get the Valley boy pickins: tattooed rocker types, trucker lugs, nerdy lightweights, and a bounty of beer bellied old men. As is pretty much always the case, the earlier you go in, the more mature the crowd, so unless you have grandchildren, check out the Starlite later at night, when the "youth" shines brightest.

LOS ANGELES'S BEST DIVE BARS

Tonga Hut

12808 Victory Blvd.
Phone: (818) 769-0708

From 1958 through 2005, this kitschy North Hollywood dive provided a liquored-up luau vibe for both cocktail culture enthusiasts and valley alkies who wouldn't have known a tiki from a totem. Indeed for many, Tonga's tropics odes were incidental to its location, cheap drinks and amusingly retro regulars (and I'm talking real retro, as in walkers and hearing aids). This was mostly due to its dilapidated state. The tiki-torch splendor of the bar's heydey, when owners Abe and Ed Libby were on the forefront of the umbrella-adorned fruit drink trend, had burnt itself out by the eighties and nineties, and while the bar remained a fave with Polynesia loving peeps, see-and-be- scenesters and bar crowds in general, were few and far between.

Then, in 2005, Tonga fans Jeremy Fleener and Ana Reyes (both of whom have a connection with the rap group Cypress Hill) decided to buy LA's oldest still-open tiki bar and return it to its former glory. They didn't swankify to the point of unrecognition like some new owners do, nor did they stuff the place with chotch-kees like the similarly tropical Tiki Ti (see Silver Lake). The changes were subtle but significant: they repaired the broken fountain (aka "the drooling bastard"), scoured the formerly crusty kidney-shaped drop ceiling, brought back the Polynesian masks and velvet paintings as well as the room's mascot of sorts, a 7-foot-tall *moai* (Easter Island statue). They also programmed the jukebox with the kind of soundtrack the new crowds would definitely appreciate (Exotica, Rockabilly, and Lounge sounds plus some sprinklings of eighties rock, classic rock and R&B and hip hop).

Five years later, the hut is a hoppin' hula-hub brimming with fashionable Valley girls and boys, hotrod-lovin' greaser types and their crimson-lipped Bettie Page lookalike dates, and casual cocktailers from all over town looking for a lay, uh, lei. The Tonga Lei to be exact, made with crème de banana, coconut nectar, rum and clove liqueur. That one will have you drooling like a bastard all right. Other colorfully-named, pack-a-punch concoctions worth their price tags ($5-$10) include the Ginger Flame, Tonga Punch, Rhumboogie, Cum in a Hot tub (shot), and mandatory Zombies and Blue Hawaiians. For the tolerance-challenged, I suggest sticking to the PBR on tap (only a buck on certain nights). If you do partake in the fresh-fruit embellished bitches brews here, prepare to call a taxi, as most of 'em are stronger than a Samoan on steroids.

MORE DIVING IN THE VALLEY

Oxwood Inn 13713 Oxnard St. Van Nuys. Phone: (818) 997-9666

Irelands 32 13721 Burbank Blvd. Van Nuys. Phone: (818) 785-4031

Pat's Cocktails 12121 Riverside Dr. North Hollywood. Phone: (818) 761-7340

Michael's Pub 11506 Oxnard St. North Hollywood. Phone: (818) 980-9762

The Barrel 4547 Van Nuys Blvd. Sherman Oaks. Phone: (818) 990-2095

Stovepiper Lounge 19563 Parthenia St. Northridge. Phone: (818) 886-2526

Lee's 17040 Devonshire St. Northridge. Phone: (818) 360-8893

Golden Nugget 4435 Cochran St. Simi Valley. Phone: (805) 583-9715

BURBANK

Blue Room

916 S San Fernando Blvd.
Phone: (323) 849-2779

Dive Bar Rating

Though bordering Burbank and Glendale, two cities known more for their malls than anything else (adjacent shopping meccas The Glendale Galleria, The Americana, The Burbank Mall, and a gargantuan IKEA store are landmarks), The Blue Room offers a relaxing oasis that couldn't feel further away from the modern retail-whirl nearby. The bar melds Rat Pack-ish retro style with a contemporary groove, a blend that's the result of various remodels, each an update with nods to its previous incarnation.

The Blue Room opened its doors sometime in the '40s, and owner John Samarjian's family have had the place since 1950 (According to Samarjian, after a fire in '52, they rebuilt the bar with a post-modern guise). John took over after his mom passed away in '82 and made his own changes, namely making the moniker a literal one, with all-blue hues inside and out. The Samarjians by the way, were big libation lovers; they owned a slew of downtown bars in the '40s, all with jazzy names like Torch Club, Fig Leaf, The 422, Swing Time and the still standing—but sold off—Valley dive The Foxfire. Like the Blue Room itself, those bars attracted the names of the era, including Jayne Mansfield and prizefighters such as Jack Dempsey, a pal of John's dad (The pair is pictured together in a prominent spot on the Blue Room's wall).

Shiny turquoise booths that are well-maintained but definitely not new, bachelor pad accents, and coordinating azure lighting illuminate the entire room, creating an almost aquarium-like feel. If I had any doubt before, I am convinced now: blue is a very soothing color. Of course, the brick-stiff booze (cash only, natch) might be part of the chill thrill too. It definitely feels like a flashbacky breath of fresh air walking in, even when hip-hop is on the sound system. There's more to look at in the lush back patio and on the roof of the place in the back parking lot: a strange elephant sculpture shooting a gun, done by a sculptor pal of Samajian's and inspired by the LA "freeway shooter" of 2005. Also of note is the entrance to the bar, which boasts an unusual furrowed steel exterior and great old fashioned neon signage, both blue-hued of course. No surprise that this moody, modish room (which Samajian's insists is "not a dive, it's a joint!") has been seen in many films over the years, namely the time-trippy *Memento*, Michael Mann's *Heat* and the neo-gangster hit sequel, *The Whole 10 Yards*.

Sardo's

259 N Pass Ave.
Phone: (818) 846-8126

Dive Bar Rating

Dirk Digler would feel right at home at this Burbank mini-mall dive, sandwiched between an Italian eatery and a Bank of America. While the Mark Wahlberg character in *Boogie Nights* wasn't a real person (supposedly he was an amalgamation of seventies era porn stars including the deceased John Holmes) if he was, and was still alive today, he'd probably look like a lot of the 50-something regulars at Sardos. Leathery skin, toupees, 'staches. On second thought, the men here are more Jack Horner-like, the Burt Reynolds director character in the epic Paul Thomas Anderson film, one of my all time favorite movies for its retro ambiance and insider depiction of the San Fernando Valley lifestyle.

The Valley and adjacent Burbank are still well known porn hubs, and driving through these sunny neighborhoods, it's easy to forget the salaciousness that goes down behind the doors of many of its manicured homes. This underbelly—not to mention the cleavage—is exposed inside Sardos. The girls are big-boobed and anything but fresh-faced, except for the barmaids who actually look young and untarnished, though awkward and obvious in very, very low-cut t-shirts brandished with the Sardos name.

It should be noted that I am judging the bar by its most popular night, a promotion called "Porn Star Karaoke" (or "PSK Tuesdays" as it's discreetly referred to on the Sardos website) which packs the place every Tuesday. While Sardos has different themes nearly every night of the week—Rockband 2 (Monday), Pop Quiz Team Trivia (Wednesday), NFL Breakfast (Sunday) and even Family Karoke (Friday from 7-9:30 p.m.)—"PSK Tuesdays" is not only the wildest night, but makes best use of the bar's cheestastic backdrop, which includes four gargantuan greasy looking lamp contraptions hanging from the ceiling and striped wall-paper behind the giant TV screens (there are several); all sooo '70s. There is ample, restaurant style seating inside but on Tuesdays anyway, it's all reserved for "the industry" as the big, scary Sumo wrestler looking bouncer explained as he pointed to the rear bar area where non-professionals like myself were relegated behind a wooden and brass post lined partition. Elbow-room deficient and forced to peer through the head-sized openings of said post to view the bad, only moderately sexy crooning, the vibe is lively but the squish factor ultimately becomes too much. Horny dudes who obviously came here to hook-up inevitably initiate vapid conversation (you are squeezed up against them after all) and the singing gets worse as the night wears on, even if the gals who come in later are hotter and more fun to watch, and free adult material is up for grabs.

BURBANK

LOS ANGELES'S BEST DIVE BARS

Tin Horn Flats

2623 W Magnolia Blvd.
Phone: (818) 567-2470

Squeaky saloon doors that swing—and just might slap ya in the ass—as you enter, a sunset-hued sign that's like something out of a movie set, and barn-like wood-beamed interior touches make this sassy saloon, which proudly boasts being "Burbank's oldest neighborhood watering hole- since 1939" worth moseying through if only for a look and a little horsing around.

It might be in one of the sleepier parts of the Burb, but Flats friendly, high-flyin' feel, amped up by games on the tube, a lively jukebox and a pool table in the front of the place (opposed to the back room like most bars) makes it a humdinger most nights. Guys in matching sports jerseys flock here (after their local "league" games no doubt) as do couples on dates (nothing like a campy environment and well-made vodka cran to break the ice). Many of the regulars do seem to know each other, hollering back and forth and joining each other to grab a smoke out front, so entering this one as a newbie can make you feel a bit like the lonesome stranger in a bad western flick. Rest assured, however, that no matter how old timey it looks, this aint the kind of place where you will see a lot of bar brawls or good-guy/bad-guy showdowns. The 'tenders are nice and they pour nice (having recently switched back from electronically measured to hand pours), plus they've a great namesake brew, Tin Horn Blonde, on tap and the pitchers are cheap ($12). Saddle up your stomach before trying the food menu though, as this gulch's grub is greasy and it can leave you hee(ve)-hawing after a visit.

Big Fish

GLENDALE

Big Fish

5230 San Fernando Rd.
Phone: (818) 244-6442

Everything you wanna know about the Big Fish is conveniently crammed together on laminated menu-sized cards copiously placed throughout the bar. Or so that's what bartender JP Lagloive (also an owner) told me repeatedly upon my first visit. When did it open? He points to the Fish "tail" (get it?) section on the card. Entertainment? Points to the schedule on the back of the same card. Any specialty drinks? "It's on the card!" he said a little impatiently. From this initial exchange, my companions and I gathered that JP wasn't a terribly chatty fellow, but after hanging out for a while, we changed our minds. Eventually, he was talking up a storm with a guy nursing a Heineken a few stools away, and after a while he seemed to warm up to us as well. We were obvious newbies, and this is one of those clubhouse-like drinking establishments, the ones that often get *Cheers* references, however cliché (one bartender, an older gent with a New York accent, was even dubbed the "Sam Malone" of Glendale by a local paper). Clearly, everyone really does know everyone's name here.

The multitude of nautical knick-knacks and the room's dark n' dusty nooks (a tiny stage for karaoke, comedy, and occasional bands; a mini-library packed with dog-eared paperbacks and board games with missing pieces), make it feel like a family den, the room where dad put all his fishin' collectables and stuff. A seemingly never-at rest pool table is anchored in the middle of the room and a giant marlin hangs on the back wall (the "big fish" from which the place got its name originally, JP told me... that was not on the card, by the way). Here's what is: In 1940 the building went up; from 1966 through 1980 it was a beer bar called The Tiger's Den (according to my dad who went there, a real dump); in 1980 new owners came in and renamed it Big Fish. The Lagloive family, which includes JP, sisters Michele and Rene, have owned it since July 9, 1999. It seems the Fish knows more than its regular's names, too, as the card also features a list of "customer birthdays" alongside limericks from JP's dad. Unlike the bar itself, the card gets updated every month.

Corner Bar

924 S San Fernando Blvd.
Phone: (818) 845-1861

Dive Bar Rating

This Glendale/Burbank bordered booze house (yes, it's on a corner) shares the block and a parking lot with the decidedly snazzier Blue Room. While the Corner lacks Blue's exotic flavor, that seems to be a plus for many of the less-trendy locals who frequent it. Laid back and shamelessly plain, the bar's warm-toned crimson paint job is about all that stands out, that and the staff of friendly barmaids who cheerily chat up even the scummiest barstool buster (Roxy, who even has her own signature drink on the menu, is a saint). Corner may not be the most distinctive establishment, but the drinks will put a lot of hair on your chest for very little ($5-$6 range).

The place has gone through several transformations over the years: salsa club, strip joint, gay bar, Thai chick pick-up joint. The last few were under the snazzy spelled moniker, Razzberriez, and if you look closely you can still see that name on the forest green awning outside. The owners attempts at covering it were half-assed at best, an approach that seems to go for the place in general. Bare minimum style, cash only, spacious, cement smoking patio out back, just-okay selection of classic rock, soul and pop hits on the jukebox (which I should note is digital, as are most dive bar jukes these days), and a menu that meshes the traditional greasy fried fare of your average bar with the traditional greasy fried food of the Orient (the owners are Asian). Recommended Corner Bar pairing: ice old beer and pot stickers.

Dave's

708 E Broadway
Phone: (818) 956-9123

Dive Bar Rating

I really hate it when people say that something is so "un LA," as if there is one blanket approach or attitude that represents the entire City of Angels. However, this description is appropriate at Dave's. Walking into the place, which has stood on the same stretch of Broadway in Glendale since the '30s, you really feel like you're somewhere in the Midwest. Things just seem to move at a slower pace here, at least on early weeknights and during happy (nappy?) hour, when some of the fellas look downright dazed. The smallish room—which surrounds you with familiar wood paneling and red tints—has long been a meat and potatoesy American dad kind of bar, the type of place that Al Bundy, Archie Bunker, or Dan Connor might frequent after a hard days work to shoot some pool (there's one table) and imbibe their favorite poison.

But this vibe is changing, and these days Dave's can be a real gumbo of Glendalers on certain nights. New owners came in a few years ago, and though they didn't do much to transform the look of the space (it was cleaned up a bit interior-wise, but the old neon outside was simply refurbished), they did start offering lively promotions like Karaoke (Fridays), live blues on Saturdays, and live jazz (Mondays). The acts range from not so great Billie Holiday wanna-be's (they'll make ya melancholy, but for the wrong reasons) to really good jazz trios and soloists appropriate for a much bigger, fancier room. The old fatherly figures still file in on Tuesdays, when bartender Pete, a fifty-ish gent known for sporting a spiffy white shirt and black tie ensemble behind the bar, transforms the place into his own old timey den party with free pool and pizza, and mellow rock music from cassette tapes he pops into a boombox.

LOS ANGELES'S BEST DIVE BARS

Winchester Room

6522 San Fernando Rd.
Phone: (818) 241-5475

Dive Bar Rating

▲▲▲▲▲

Scuffed furniture, dusty liquor bottles, and an incongruent array of "art" are dive bar traits one notices again and again. Though The Winchester has all of these, it's another kind of feature altogether that make it an archetypal LA dive: the regulars. Slip into this ancient Glendale grotto, hidden inside a lackluster mini-mall on any day of the week after six or so, and you will come upon a cast of characters that even more than Big Fish up the street, recall the TV show *Cheers*, only not as light-hearted.

Though fun to sip and talk snide with, it wont escape you that these are the kinds of daily drinkers you might see on the TV show *Intervention*, the ones who refuse help even though their teary families are begging them stop the sauce. There's George, or as the barmaids call him, "Uncle George" a Cliff Clavin know-it-all type who attempted to tell me the history of the bar in between eyeing *Jeopardy* on the TV. George has his own personal glass, which gets filled up with beer non-stop by his "nieces." (He leaves it in the bar after each visit). As George gets more inebriated, he gets louder and more animated, and even a bit antagonistic if you disagree with him about something. "I know everything, damn it!" he shouts with a smile, but in a still quite serious tone. Then there's Fred, whom you'll probably know all about before he even walks in the door, as the others reference him frequently, as one might refer to an uncle at a family gathering. Fred also has his own glass behind the bar, a gold-leafed, Asian-style tea mug, which gets filled with ice cubes and beer the moment he walks in. Fred's seen three different owners come through the Winchester, and though the current owner is Chinese, he credits the previous Thai management with starting the personal mug thing. "I joked that they were gonna turn the bar all Thai in here," he said. "The next day the manager, being a smart ass, brought this in for me. I've been drinking from it ever since."

Fred seemed to know the most about the Winchester's background. He told me that the place was named after the vintage firearm, opening in the '50s with a Western theme and cowboy touches like John Wayne pictures and gun replicas. As it's gone through different owners over the years, the look of the place has become a hodge-podge of décor sensibilities (blue walls, red booths, mirrors). The current owner, Jin Pak (many of the regulars call him "Jim"), obviously likes music; he added pictures of Madonna, Bob Marley and John Lennon to the offbeat mix, plus a digital jukebox. Karaoke on weekends sees a more energetic vibe than you'll encounter on a weeknight pow-wow. Despite slightly younger visitors on weekends, this may be one of the few alky holes in LA that remains undercover forever, as its location is well concealed and its mature regulars too intense and entrenched. The Winchester might be an amusing place for a random laugh and a bargain buzz (beers are $3 and mixed drinks $4-$5), but I can't see trendy types ever camping out here.

GLENDALE

LOS ANGELES'S BEST DIVE BARS

Tony's Bar
1300 S. Brand Blvd.
Phone: (818) 241-1891

Dive Bar Rating

So drearily ordinary I'm almost at loss for words to describe it, Tony's is nonetheless a dive that thrives in the Glendale area, strangely perched amongst a slew of car dealerships and not much else. From its too common moniker (there may be a "Tony's" in every city; there's at least two in this book) to its lackluster look (the usual wood paneling, cracked vinyl seating, pool tables specked with bald spots, and cob-webbed corners) this bar would have absolutely no mojo if it weren't for the odd mix of patrons who seem to frequent it.

While the rarely empty, fairly spacious room found along "auto row," as some call this stretch of Brand Blvd., unsurprisingly attracts after work car dealer crews drinking away the frustrations from less than stellar sales (especially lately), there's also a sizeable Spanish speaking slew, which is surprising since this part of Glendale is populated mainly by Armenians and whites. Tony's does get its share of white winos as well, usually drinking solo and often engaged in anything but the place itself (napkin scribblers, newspaper readers and even iPod wearers attempting to block out the often throbbingly loud Latin dance beats). There's also a consistent WTF element, as in "what the... females"? For Glendale gals of a certain age, this lowly, grey room seems to be a goldmine for getting their guy groove on, and the times I ventured inside, I couldn't help but eye the colorfully ensembled ladies sipping seductively at the bar. One gal wore yellow from head to toe (including shoes, bag and hat) while another was adorned in piles of Mr. T-like gold jewelry. A sure way to get noticed, sure, but lucky? I've never stayed long enough to find out.

Tops Club

4227 San Fernando Rd.
Phone: (818) 246-0982

For years, I have driven past by this bar with no sign, as it stands on busy San Fernando Rd., the street that takes me from my pad in Silver Lake to my parents place further North. The plain corner bricked establishment wouldn't have ever caught my attention if it weren't for its consistently swung open side door's beckoning black and white sign ("no one under 21 admitted") suggesting that either stripping or sipping was going down inside.

One day I finally sauntered in, hoping not to be noticed too much. Turns out that no amount of sauntering would have saved me from sticking out, as the Tops Club is a full-on Mexicano bar, the kind where the only Ingles you'll find on the jukebox is Shakira, all the beers are Latin-branded (Tecate, Dos Equis, Negra Modelo, Corona, and ok, Budweiser too), and free Menudo is served every Tuesday. I happened to be there on a Tuesday, but didn't try the Menudo (which for those who don't know, is not just the boy band that bore Ricky Martin and Rico Suave, but is also a spicy Mexican soup made with tripe…interestingly, it's considered to be quite the hangover remedy). The waitresses were really nice, if really badly and trashily dressed, and the one who spoke English the best gave me the low-down on the place. The cash only bar has been here for over thirty years, has never had a sign, and only offers cerveza. All of the bottled and canned brews are served with lime and a packet of salt, something I've never seen done so consistently anywhere else. A gal sitting next to me coated the rim of her bottle with the granules, so I followed suit, loved it, and have been pretending my Coronas are Margaritas ever since. Two pool tables, too bright lighting, and décor that consists of nothing more than some sepia-toned Mexican Revolutionary photos and a tower of Cup O' Noodles make the Tops Club (cleavage-bearing barmaids notwithstanding) nearly as plain inside as it is out.

Where Else, Inc?

SUNLAND
and
LA CRESCENTA

The Sundown

7803 Foothill Blvd
Phone: (818) 352-5792

The stretch of Foothill Blvd. that spans La Crescenta to Sunland might not be that far from the more popular drinking areas featured in this book (it's a mere 15 minutes—as is almost everything in Los Angeles, or so goes the joke—via the 2 freeway from Hollywood/downtown), but it feels like it's a world away. A surreal experience is guaranteed at any of the bars in the area, but I suggest a car crawl to all four listed here, with The Sundown as the main attraction.

A hog-rider haven that's seen its share of dregs and drugs (a sign asking patrons to kindly refrain from "illegal substances" greets you at the door and a bulletin board has fliers for bail bonds), The Sundown is a raucous redneck roadhouse with character, as well as some real grizzly characters, all of whom are kept in check by burly security and the friendly but badass bartender. This busty broad wears Harley tees and jeans two sizes too snug, swears like a sailor and pours like a siren as she chats with regulars about the latest drunken drama that went down a couple nights previous (some ASSHOLE hit a bike parked in the lot with his GODDAMNED pick-up truck). There's the older, Aqua-net sprayed lady getting sauced on MGD, whose voice gains more volume with each chug (quote before her wobbly exit: "All the men who come here are pricks!"). And then there's the lanky Kid Rock-ish fella in a wife-beater singing along to songs on the jukebox as if he's auditioning for a heavy metal choir. When Sublime's "April 26, 1992"—about the LA riots—comes on, he busts out with blaring zeal: *"They said it was for the black man/They said it was for the Mexican/And not for the white man/But if you look at the streets it wasn't about Rodney King/ It's about this fucked up situation and these fucked up police/It's about coming up and staying on top and screamin' 187 on a mother fuckin' cop!"* Not exactly feel-good bar music, but kind of fitting, 'cause to put it bluntly, this is a Reginald Denny kind of place. I'm actually surprised to hear the Long Beach ska-punk band on the soundsystem since browsing the jukebox it's all Wayland Jennings, Janis Joplin and Skynard. 'Cycle gangs take over on certain nights, especially on Wednesdays, which is Weasels night ("a drinking club with a motorcycle problem," according to their website). With a pool table, dart boards and an adjacent room full of video games, there's plenty to keep patrons occupied at The Sundown, but be prepared; even when they're engaged in harmless activities, these handle-bar lovin' buffsters can be hard to handle.

SUNLAND & LA CRESCENTA

Famous LA Divers

Charles Bukowski

Frank Sinatra

Vince Vaughn

David Lynch

Quentin Tarantino

Kiefer Sutherland

LOS ANGELES'S BEST DIVE BARS

Where else, Inc?

8234 Foothill Blvd.
Phone: (818) 352-0550

Dive Bar Rating

Let me employ the bar's not exactly nuanced name to tell ya about this one. Where have I seen a very pale, ginger-haired 100 lb guy with a flat-top hair-cut show off his abs? *Where else?* Where did I hear an inebriated college co-ed, feeling all "Girls Gone Wild," on tequila shots, ask the biker babe bartender if she could, please, please slap her ass? *Where else?* Where did I see a Wrangler jeaned booty thrust obligingly over the bar counter for aforementioned lushy young lady to slap? *Where else?*

In a space that once housed The Sundown—and sharing some of the same regulars—this murky hideaway has its own "born to be wild" vibe, complete with Harley wall art, tiny toy cycles parked throughout the liquor bottle stock, and a younger, hotter version of Sundown's 'tender (her clothes are tight, but at least they fit). Wearing a tee that ironically says, "Hands Off My Lucky Charms," you get the feeling that this gal gets her ass slapped a lot in here... and she likes it. The room, your typical wood-paneled hut with one pool table, a dart board and a juke pumping out Stones, Segar and "Alcoholica" (as the skinny dude hoots when "Enter Sandman" comes on), is nothing to look at, but it feels surprisingly cozy, like Sundown's cuter little sister. However, it can get loud, as the crowd are the type to chant along with the music (*"Exit Light, Enter Night, Take My Hand, Off to Never-neverland"...* yeah!) The staff seem a lot more lax then those up the street; hence, lazies and crazies too juiced to jet out back for a smoke sometimes bust out the Camels and Kools on their stools right inside the bar, sans reprimand. The management does draw the line at weed and other mood enhancers though, which are done strictly, *where else?*, outside.

Whisperz

3645 Foothill Blvd
Phone: (818) 957-9919

Dive Bar Rating

Two words sum up this peculiar, punky li'l liquor pit: Korn karaoke. Yes, Whisperz is a karaoke bar—says so on its colorful neon sign—so you'll find some of the usual cuckoo for coco-puffs crooners of all ages and walks of life popping in to torture the staff with off-key renditions of Phil Collins and Billy Joel. For the most part, though, most of Whisperz's aggro-alkies aren't hip enough to even think about *Wedding Singer*-esque retro rock hero homage's on the mic. Instead, for these faux-hawked, backward baseball capped hell-raisers, it's metal and grunge, a total '90's rewind in which Korn's "Got the Life" gets a fist-pump behind the bar from the porn-starish pourer, who wears a vinyl mini skirt, bra-baring fishnet tee and blonde hair with black roots. She looks bored if the music aint blaring, and Hole's "Violet" inspires grrrl power in the form of bodyshots (Whisperz's signature drink is called "Blue Balls." 'Nuff said).

While it might sound like I'm being derogatory, the truth is that this place is a gas and the lack of pretense is refreshing. They've got the FUSE music channel on the giant TV screen behind the bar and games scattered about—especially loved the x-rated Jenga tower with hand written commands like "grab the guy's nuts next to you" and " flash your tits" on each piece. This is the Fred Durst of bars, especially on "Tubetop Tuesdays" a long and very loud night. Live bands on weekends (safe bet they've all got dreads and facial piercings), free pool and beer pong ("don't forget to wash your balls") and all the time specials like $3 Jager and Crown bombs and $1 Kamikaze shots will make your memory of Whisperz the next day anything but a gentle murmur.

Up Th' Hill

2856 Foothill Blvd.
Phone: (818) 957-9997

The most depressing place on the Sunland/La Crescenta sipper stretch, Up The Hill, which is, you got it, up Foothill's northern side, looks from the outside like its been closed for several years: darkened windows, unlit sign, etc. Once you open the door to this den of down and out inequity and walk inside, things don't look much different; sour-faced fifty-somethings sipping whisky on the rocks while watching ESPN and (interestingly) The History Channel, and a bartender who looks like he'd rather be anywhere else. The Hill is the epitome of the insulated regulars bar and outsiders can't help but stand out like a peacock in a chicken coop, so prepare for stank-eye if you are a first timer, under fifty or have on anything even remotely trendy clothing-wise. So why would you want to hang with the sloshed slags and mostly retired drunkards here? The drinks of course, which are bargain-priced ($3-$5) and (high) ballsy as hell. A decaying pool table, old, ill-placed TV sets, and a crock pot serving up mystery stews on certain nights seem to be the most exciting amusements at Up Th' Hill (if there's a jukebox, I didn't notice it). You may not find your thrill here, but at least you'll hold on to your bills while getting' a good buzz.

The 35er

PASADENA

The 35er

12 E Colorado Blvd.
Phone: (626) 356-9315

Old Town Pasadena is indeed old, but the most popular businesses clustered along its busiest stretch—Colorado between Pasadena Avenue on the west and the Arroyo Parkway on the east— are anything but. After it was designated a historic district in the early '80s, the area became a commercial Mecca brimming with upscale eateries, chain restaurants and familiar storefronts that continue to thrive today.

The authentic vintage neon sign outside of the 35er—which claims the distinction of being the oldest bar in Pasadena—may not fit in exactly, but it does contribute to the visual ebullience of the area. The space, which is also known as Freddie's 35-er and which locals call the "dirty diver," isn't all that dirty or divey. It's more of an unruly sports bar, with memorabila (mostly Dodger jerseys and plaques) smattered about, games on multiple screens and animated fans adding comments or curses to the play by play. Pasadena is a sports town in many ways, especially around college bowl season in January when the nearby Rose Bowl hosts some big games, and the world-famous Tournament of Rose Parade fills the boulevard with marching bands and cheerleaders from all around the country on New Years Day. Colorado is parade-like almost every weekend, in fact, and no where is the energy more rabid than at this sloppy-fun spot, which opens up its dingy, dungeon-like downstairs area when it gets really crowded, even bringing in DJs to pump the peeps with hip-hop and dance hits. Nice tap selection and cheap—for pricey Pasadena—cocktails ($5-$6), plus an always brimming free popcorn machine, the kernels of which seem to get everywhere: on the floor, on the pool tables (there are two), in the stool cracks and after my last visit, in my bra (you don't wanna know).

Colorado Bar

2640 E Colorado Boulevard
Phone: (626) 449-3485

If you're doing the Colorado dive crawl (by car or cab, as the three bars listed here are too far from each other to do it by foot), the Colorado Bar will likely end up as your favorite. The atmosphere is cool, but not too cool, the hues dark but not murky (even with blacked out windows) and the crowd is a grab bag of punky locals, aged freaks, and people that you can't quite peg one way or the other. (I mean grab bag literally, because some pals of mine have been groped when it got crowded on weekends). Like many bars in this book, it's the weeknights that have a more slacker, less wackster appeal, as prehistoric Pasadena alkies sit at the bar while creatively coiffed twentysomethings from the nearby Art Center university camp out in the booths on the opposite side of the room, seemingly deep in conversation about surrealism or something, but not so deep that they're oblivious to every person who walks in the front door.

The bar's been around since 1964, and though it's under different ownership now, it's still just as grimy good as during the ol' days. The peeling bordello-esque flocked wallpaper still reeks of cig stench from when they were looser about puffing indoors, and the newer touches—a wall art collage featuring an assemblage of classic album covers such as The Rolling Stones' *Black and Blue*, The Beatles' *Abbey Road*, Madonna's *Like A Virgin*, and the *Saturday Night Fever* soundtrack—give the place a dorm-ish rock n' roll edge, as well as some ideas for what to choose on the CD jukebox (they've got all the classics you could want, though not a lot of new stuff). Mismatched chairs that appear to be bought at a coffeehouse closeout sale provide ample seating in the back room next to the pool tables, where you must put your name down on a chalkboard to play, even if no one else is waiting. According to the owner, a simultaneously surly and sweet white haired fellow, "Some asshole might take your turn!" A no BS bar in an area known for affluent residents and franchise frenzied businesses, this place puts the "rad" in Colo-rad-o.

R Place

3739 E Colorado Blvd
Phone: (626) 792-7330

Dive Bar Rating

If the 35er is sporty and the Colorado Bar is arty, than R Place would best be labeled crusty, at least clientele-wise. When I was at the Colorado and mentioned that I was headed to the R Place, a regular at the former gave me a disheartened look and taunted "Oh, you wanna see where the hookers and addicts drink, do ya?" This statement may have been made more of loyalty to the 'Rado than an actual warning, as the R Place isn't that ominous. While misfits and lowlifes do occasionally gravitate here, especially later in the evening, for the most part, the bar is comprised of locals, mainly trucker-ish men, bloated and blasted fifty-something ladies and young guys who like to sip their MGD and Buds in peace, i.e., an empty room, as R Place rarely gets crowded.

Roll into the big R to get smashed out of your gourd, to play pool and bar games without a wait or to win the lottery (and I'm not talking about hooking up). A giant kiosk for the Cali lottery stands conspicuously in the corner of the bar, taunting the downers and outers who dwell here with the possibility of hitting it rich. A lot of bars have lottery gaming, but none as in your face as it is here and it's surprising we don't see more of these big ugly things in more bars. Thankfully, you don't need a jackpot to gulp here. The prices are as reasonable ($5 for a basic cocktail) as they should be, even if the strength of the mixes are related to how well the 'tender knows you, not to mention his/her mood that day. That said, the guys and gals who work here are obviously beloved by their boozers ("Sergio," "Jana" Chuck " and "Shannon" each have their own cute, kind of out of place hand-painted sign behind the bar). They may not know everybody's name, but everybody knows theirs.

MORE DIVING NEARBY:

1818 Bar 1881 E Washington Blvd Pasadena. Phone: (626) 794-3068
Rancho Bar 2485 N Lake Ave. Altadena. Phone: (626) 798-7634
The Buccaneer 70 W Sierra Madre Blvd. Sierra Madre. Phone: (626) 355-9045

LOS ANGELES'S BEST DIVE BARS

5006

Johnny's

EAST LA/SAN GABRIEL VALLEY

Whittier
Rosemead
Highland Park
Boyle Heights

Embers Lounge

11332 Washington Blvd.
Phone: *(562) 699-4138*

Dive Bar Rating

🍾🍾🍾🍾

Approximately twelve miles southeast of Los Angeles, Whittier might not be the destination most would choose for a wild night out on the town. At least not these days. In the '70s and '80s, however, Whittier Blvd. was a prime spot for cruising, a veritable parade of hot rods and lowriders that attracted customized auto-lovers from all over the city. Following crackdowns from the local coppers over the years, this isn't the case anymore, and the people I know who live near the area (even those with cool cars) tend to commute into LA proper for their nightlife fix. But for dive heads, the twenty minute drive from downtown to this somewhat sleepy suburb is an absolute must, as two of Los Angeles' most unforgettable old watering holes (both under the same ownership) happen to be within a block of each other on a stretch of Washington Blvd.

Ember's has all the dive essentials: warm, lumpy leatherette booths, pool tables with balls so old the paint is chipping off (they're made to be hit, so that's saying something), one of those sexy old souvenir dispensers in the bathroom (four quarters yields a sticker with a blush-worthy limerick I won't write here and a tiny pamphlet featuring pictures of "Sexual Positions From Around The World"), and bartenders with voices like sandpaper and personalities as soft as tissue paper, friendly even to obvious outsiders/gawkers.

So what's to gawk at, you ask? Simply put, it's the art. California artist Frank Bowers was obviously inspired by the bar's scorching moniker, as his mystically moody oil works of topless Hollywood starlets as devils in Hades-like settings fill the place—there's two big pieces behind the bar and individual pieces above each booth. Bowers, whose mural work graces South Gate City Hall and dive bars alike (his less malevolent works can still be seen at The Buccaneer Bar in Sierra Madre and the Foc'sle Bar in Wilmington) may not have had a gift for portraiture (Marilyn Monroe and Kirk Douglas are recognizable, but Natalie Wood, Jayne Mansfield and Rock Hudson not so much) but he did have an imposing stroke style and knack for alluring atmosphere that recalled old pulp novel covers. The

horny, breast-baring babes at Embers were arguably his masterpieces. Though he died in '64, soon after he created them, his bar work
(which he supposedly did to pay off his tabs) lives on. At Embers,
they do more than that: they inspire a new generation of hellhounds
to drink themselves one step closer to eternal damnation.

WHITTIER

LOS ANGELES'S BEST DIVE BARS

Poor Denny's Saloon

8020 Boer Ave.
Phone: (562) 695-4090

Dive Bar Rating

P.Denny's boasts a nostalgic nautical theme complete with fish and pelican statues and plaques, paintings of perfect storm-style ship voyages (not by Frank Bowers unfortunately), and blue and red lighting that represents actual boating navigation signals. There's also a groovy aquarium tank filled with finned ones and turtles... turtles that don't exactly get along, providing hours of entertainment as they swipe at each other while you sit at the bar, submerging yourself in cheap drinks ($4.50-$5). It's another "lottery bar," with a big kiosk right next to the jukebox so that you can choose your numbers while you are choosing your tunes. The music is shockingly eclectic, with everything from The Misfits to Morrissey to Smashing Pumpkins to Patsy Cline.

While subtly punky, mostly twentysomething Latino crews seem to control the soundtrack, an entirely different kind of mob sits motionless at the bar stools, mainly bleary eyed older folk who give off a fear and loathing of unfamiliar faces energy. This awkward, you don't belong here vibe is nothing a couple of cocktails can't remedy, and P.D. is smooth sailing after about an hour's drinking, where a rapport with your fellow patrons can be forged, if you so desire. The 'tendress was even kind enough to warn me about a bar across the street I was considering checking out called The Stein. It's a no-go, she said, "unless you don't speak English and like ladies with brown pantyhose and white pumps." Even though this description applies to a few of the bars in this book (Tops Club, One Eye Jack) I decided to pass and simply keep Whittier as a terrific two-fer.

Spike's

7813 Garvey Ave.
Phone: (626) 288-4366

This faux wood-panel and poster-plastered bar and billiards spot is a favorite with East L.A.'s rockabilly and greaser types, which means that the parking lot is often packed with gleaming, cherried-out vintage autos. But the cars (and the hair) are about the only thing that still gleam at this worn-in yet warm wreck n' roll room, and that's the way the regulars (young and old) like it. Pungent cig stench, tenuous toilets (a sign warns gals in the ladies room not to flush anything, even toilet paper), loutish bartenders and all, Spike's rawness seems to be part of its appeal for the retro-roughs who frequent it after dark.

Spike's wasn't always a fashionable rock rumble. The place has been around since the WWII-era, when the area flourished with drinking holes. Bartender and head booker Brandon Terrazas, aka club promoter Brando Von Badsville, who is responsible for bringing the younger rocker set to the place, says that plenty of its original regulars, many whom now live in nearby nursing homes, still loaf here by day, reminiscing about the ol' days. As a result, he's been privy to many heated disagreements about the bar's history. "The old daytimers mention two previous names before breaking off into tangents and blurred memories," chuckles Terrazas, who says there is no paper trail to settle arguments about the place. "Supposedly it was called the Dew Drop in 1948 which was a post military slang name for "wet pussy." That name lasted until the early to mid fifties, when it was changed to Andy's Alibi, which was a burlesque bar (the first in San Gabriel Valley). Rumor has it that Andy's wife sold the bar when he was out of town one weekend as they were going through a divorce." The bar became Patrick's Cocktail Lounge in 1965 and lasted under that identity for over three decades, reinventing itself again as a cue queue in the late '80s (the adjacent pool room was added after the 1987 Whittier earthquake). Though new owners changed the name to Spike's in 1997, the moniker wasn't really simpatico with the crowd until Terrazas, a local whose grandmother used to go here, saw its potential and started booking rock bands and encouraged the owners to put in a little stage about eight years ago.

His signature night, Rev It Up!, Fridays, sees rebels from all over East LA and beyond flocking to see the bands on stage, while other nights (Wednesdays '80s music monthly, the Breakfast Klub, and the Thursday weekly, Radikal's Radio, a punk, ska, soul mash) are about the equally compact dance floor. A cover is charged on these promoter-driven nights, but the pool tables are always free, and no matter how packed the place gets, you're almost always sure to find a place for your wheels, as everybody double parks and there's never a valet taking your keys and your money like at other clubs. The door guys keep track of every auto on their lot, and will kindly, if rather loudly, give a holler inside when a vehicle needs to be moved.

MORE DIVING NEARBY:

Al's Cocktails 413 W Las Tunas Dr. San Gabriel. Phone: (626) 281-8638.

Venice Room 2428 S Garfield Ave. Monterey Park. Phone: (323) 722-3075

Jay-Dee Cafe 1843 W Main St. Alhambra. Phone: (626) 281-6887

ROSEMEAD

LOS ANGELES'S BEST DIVE BARS

Footsies

2640 N Figueroa St.
Phone: (323) 221-6900

Got a doozy of a boozy tale of yore from Footsies. Back when I was but a wee tot (the '70s), the bar happened to be my father's favorite after work watering hole. The place was called Cliff's Inn back then and the owner, an older Jewish gent by the name of Sam, was pretty tight with my pops and his co-workers. I should mention that Footsies regulars were pretty much all Spanish speaking back then, so how they communicated with Sam is beyond me. My dad, who came to the U.S. from South America as a teen was bi-lingual early on, so he probably got closer to Sam than most, and would spend hours unwinding at the bar with the feisty barkeep, who kept his regulars coming back for more by offering free drink tokens to those who cashed their hard-earned checks at the bar. Dad did just this, but one night he should've checked himself. Sam was in a good mood and bought round after round after round of Tequila Sunrises for his regulars. All my dad remembers about that evening to this day is being found sitting on the bar's commode, pants on the ground, asleep. He lost not only his head but his footing at Footsies, and had to be carried out! Talk about OG (original guzzler)… guess it's in my blood, huh?

Footsies circa the millennium has surely seen its share of blackouts too, though from a different, more boho brethren. Taken over a few years ago by Dave Neupert (Short Stop, El Chavito), Footsies, like Little Cave not far from it, has been gently gentrified. Non-English speakers still come by early for cervezas, but the gangsters, cholos and hard-working Spanish-speaking stalwarts are all but gone. Most nights it's all neo-hippie types with beards and girls in headbands and American Apparel bodysuits. Footsies has become the epitome of the "hipster dive," which means it's beloved by many and hated by some. While the place is cozy and somewhat cleaned-up from the days when daddy and Sam dwelled there, it retains a sleazy feel thanks to homey retro lighting, nude paintings on the wall, dark red and wood furniture, and Regal Beagle (the *Three's Company's* bar) style booths. Footsies is still sucking in the '70s, and if you are too, you'll dig it like I do, even without any nostalgic connections.

Johnny's

5006 York Blvd.
Phone: (323) 551-6959

Johnny's has a humongous sign that says "liquor" spanning its entire back wall. It's way too large for this smallish drinking establishment, but it works in the overall atmospheric scheme, which marries bold statements with laid back décor: simple mirrors on the entrance wall, leather chairs, a little jackalope behind the bar and monitors playing anything but sports (This aint a jock joint, it's rock joint). Vibrant, violent cartoons on the big back wall screen and classic swagger-heavy music docs like *The Song Remains The Same* flash on the TV set behind the bar most nights.

The visceral vibe of this old room—dating back to the twenties—is less about the décor, though, and more about the patrons. Johnny's has been a rockabilly, butch-chick, punker crib since it reopened in 2007. Nearly everyone in the place has ink, including the bartenders, barmaids and barbacks. My sleeve-sporting hubby and I feel right at home, but straight-laced types might be a little put off. Not that the staff here would care what you look like, if they even see you at all; Johnny's is a regulars bar, and it takes a few visits til ya really fit into the fold. If the 'tender on duty during your virgin visit seems more interested in his draft-downing dudes than your drink order, gave him a bit of 'tude when you do finally get his attention. He'll probably give you some back, but after the exchange, you should be initiated. To that end, be prepared for really loud but really good music. Whoever mixes the sounds either has kickass taste, or the best luck ever with iPod Shuffle (James Brown one minute, the Ramones the next... yes!). This li'l clubhouse may not be the roughest of the Highland Park rubs, but the crowd is revved up most nights and you don't even have to get jumped-in to join.

Little Cave

5922 N Figueroa St.
Phone: (323) 255-6871

Dive Bar Rating

As the areas of Silver Lake and Echo Park have become gentrified, twentysomethings fresh out of the family home and cheap rent seekers of all sorts have moved Eastward, so 'hoods that used to be pretty sketchy aren't so much anymore. This stretch of HP, which is also home to the divey music space Mr. T's, is probably the most obvious example. It'll never be Cahuenga Blvd. of course, but my guess is that some trendy shops and eateries will eventually follow. Til then, the street is downright serene; walking to and fro the Little Cave at night, you pass gated storefronts, easy-breezy parking, and very few street freaks.

Creatures of the night flap their wings insatiably for this pitch-black bar—and I'm not just talking about the beady-eyed varmints that hang from the sign out front. This kitschy Highland Park hideaway is a natural habitat for the vampy, tattooed types who frequent it, and it's one of the few area holes that has retained an almost mysterious if not menacing mojo despite having been madeover and covered with bats (by the guys behind Bigfoot Lodge and Saints & Sinners) in 2005. Maybe it's the quirky bartenders (some of whom blow fire and do tricks) or drink specials (Count Chocula anyone?) that give off this vibe, or maybe it's the punk rock/new wave tunes that blast during the bar's busier nights, or maybe it's the crowd itself, a hip and somewhat heavy Latino assemblage mostly, drawn from the surrounding areas of Highland Park, Glassell Park and downtown.

A couple of L.C. notes to sink your teeth into: your eyes will need to adjust to darkness in this place, even near the dance floor, where giant red globe lamps illuminate the freaky moves (weekends things can get a lil touchy-feely, so pay attention). Also, the batty bathroom is micro tiny, which means leak-seeking ladies should prepare for a long wait; if you smoke, this is the bar for you, as the outdoor patio wraps around the perimeter of the entire Halloweeny hub.

MORE DIVING NEARBY:

Dusty's 6316 York Blvd. Los Angeles, CA 90042 Phone: (323) 256-6329

Mr. T's Bowl 5621 N Figueroa St. Los Angeles, CA 90042 Phone: (323) 256-7561

Eastside Luv

1835 E 1st St.
Phone: (323) 262-7442

Where is Los Angeles' true "Eastside"? It's a debate that's filled with plenty of controversy, and for many Latino residents, outright anger. Latinos make up almost half the population of Los Angeles, and though they live all over the city, most Spanish-speaking inhabitants—and kids of Spanish speaking parents like me—grew up in areas most commonly referred to as "the Eastside." For some, the term "Eastside" has become synonymous with the Chicano movement and its struggles, but for others the term is looked upon a lot more loosely. A by-product of the city's evolving gentrification, the "Eastside" label has become attached to neighborhoods like Echo Park, Silver Lake and downtown itself, which naysayers claim is an insult to "true" Eastside communities like Montebello, Highland Park, Glassell Park and Cypress Park. While areas east of the LA River and Western Ave. like Boyle Heights, where the bar Eastside Luv is located, are also considered part of the "Eastside", the tiny bar's La Raza feel has less to do with geography and more to do with the spirited fiesta that takes place within.

Luv's barrio locale notwithstanding (it's across the street from the famed "Mariachi Plaza" where ornately dressed Mexican musicians gather for gigs), its dive vibe isn't in its decor. The place is actually quite beautiful, sort of a sexy homage to Latino and lowrider culture, complete with chandeliers done like giant chain-link car steering wheels, Dickies fabric upholstery, bordello-esque flocked falls, Mexican movie posters, a candle covered altar/fireplace (with fake log), muerto-inspired art and metal signs that read "Los Winos" above the men's room and "Las Chulas" above the chica's. Even the bar is "lowered," a sunken, dugout like hole in which 'tenders serve up wine and beer. Though the selection is limited, and there ain't no cheese (the bar's whole moniker is "Eastside Luv—wine y *queso*") there are some nice and whimsical offerings, such as the *michelada* (bloody mary mix and beer) which they jazz up with every Mexican kid's favorite liquor store staple, a *saladito* (died prune soaked in salt).

Some have taken issue with the bar's 2006 re-do (opened in

the '40s, the place was originally called Thè Metropolitan) and the "pocho"centric thrust (the term for Latinos lacking Spanish fluency), but Luv—which offers live Latin bands, burlesque and valet parking on weekends—addresses these concerns head-on via its website, which refers to the place as a leader of "gente-fication" ("gente" meaning people) and acknowledges that no matter what purists and old schoolers might say, change in a community is inevitable. As far as I am concerned, as long as a reverence for a locale's culture and past remains—and this is true for most of the refurbished joints in this book—the inner dive will thrive, and no amount of fancy wallpaper can change that.

MORE DIVING NEARBY

The Blvd 2631 Whittier Boulevard. Phone: (323) 261-3090

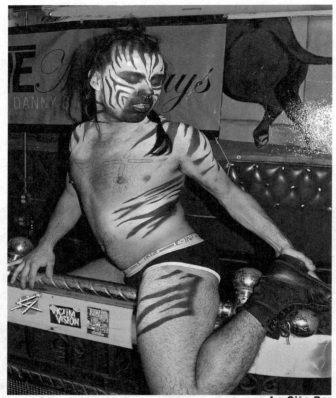

La Cita Bar

DOWNTOWN
and
DOWNTOWN ADJACENT

Little Tokyo

Chinatown

Civic Center

Angelino Heights

West Lake

Cosmos

333 E 1st St
Phone: (213) 621-2227

Cosmos is best known for its owner Joe, who's often likened to a crotchety "Japanese Elvis" because of his fifties-style pompadour hairstyle. Unfortunately, a lot of people don't love him tender, mainly because of his "Cosmos Rules," which include: no gum chewing, dancing or smoking (stogies were apparently allowed until recently); "no drinks in the bathroom;" "no sitting in reserved for karaoke tables in the back if you're not singing;" "two drink minimum" if you do plan to croon; and most importantly "no touch the equipment!" as the sign near the karaoke machine reads. Despite his often aggressive enforcement of these rules, the spunky, sixty something proprietor of this Little Tokyo karaoke bar has always been more than pleasant whenever I have popped by. The night I went in to shoot pictures for this book, for example, Joe asked to inspect the camera. Knowing his rep, I wondered to myself... *Is picture taking not allowed?* Turned out that he just wanted to admire it, and to talk about his own shutter collection. Joe might be pretty militant at times (I've seen him turn people away for having out of state IDs), but observing him is a hoot, and in my opinion, the main reason to go to Cosmos. It's his party and he can bust balls if he wants to, and truly, he does it good-naturedly most of the time.

As for the room itself, it's the polar opposite of the Far Bar a few doors down; anything but modern, and completely lacking in elan (the usual cheap Formica tables, wood paneling and handwritten signs in broken English). Both bars are on the strip known as "Ramen Row" (or as I like to refer to it, the "Sushi stroll") and make for some great post-chopstickin' sippin,' especially if you're looking for an alternative to the ubiquitous sake selections served at every other establishment in the area. Cosmos has a storefront, though it is an unusual one that looks like anything but a bar. It's got baby blue trim and two display windows, an exterior that suggests a beauty parlor or massage joint. If it weren't for the barely noticeable word "saloon" oddly placed next to "Cosmos" and some Japanese letters on the sign above outside, one could easily pass by without being aware of the musical mirth within. And there is plenty. Like most karaoke bars, the songbook contains an ample selection of classic rock (Journey, The Who, Queen) and Japanese pop, the latter of which can be as popular as the American stuff once white regulars get wasted. But not too wasted when Joe's around.

Karaoke

Backstage

Cosmos

Gaslite

Prime Time

Sardos

Smog Cutter

Far Bar

347 E 1st St.
Phone: (213) 617-9990

Quite literally a hole in the wall, the tiny, aptly named Far Bar (you have to walk down a longish, narrow brick alley to get to it) boasts a drink list that's a little too fancy and a little too pricey for its atmosphere. Still, this maroon-walled juicebox gets away with its decidedly minimalist presentation because of its locale. Far is the closest bar to the popular Geffen Contemporary extension of MOCA (Museum of Contemporary Art) and thus attracts the culture vulture set looking to ponder and pontificate post-exhibit.

It might not be deep design-wise, and it's not intentionally stark or neo-mod inclined (the interior looks like its just not quite finished yet), but the Far Bar does have a certain blank canvas appeal. The ample seating on the outdoor patio, flanked by old fire escapes from the buildings above and lit by white Christmas lights swung across, is where most convene. A couple heatlamps keep it that way during LA winters, such as they are. The sound system is usually pumping out some thumping techno music (no room for a juke here) or ambient chill grooves, and the crowd is a cordial mix of cute, often bespectacled Japanese-Americans and uber-trendy black garbed types. One might assume the fancy drinks were offered for the more pretentious tastes of museumgoers, but the selection is more inventive and whimsical than refined. The Asian Zombie is pure blue boozy bliss, on par with most tiki bar versions, and since it's filled to the brim of a pint glass, worth the $10 price tag. Other yummy sippers that bargoers seem to dig are the Far Bar Peppertini (a martini with fresh Thai chili), Oreo Outrage (Vanilla Stoli, kahlua, butterscotch, Godiva liquer, cookies and milk), and the J-Town Emperor (Crown Royal, peach Schnapps, pineapple and lime juice). The restaurant next door (same owners) offers a nice selection of sushi rolls and Japanese bar food (tempura, pot stickers), but the street out front is packed with so many Japanese food joints, many with more selection and culinary focus. Far Bar isn't for foodies, it's for faders.

Grand Star

943 N. Broadway
Phone: (213) 626-2285

Dive Bar Rating

The Grand Star dates back to 1941, and unlike most bars, it has the same name and owners (the Quon family) as it did back then. While there have been some changes over the years (most notably a small *Saturday Night Fever*-like light-up dance floor), music has always fueled this two-level bar and club. Back when it was mostly a karaoke spot, the sounds were decidedly hit or miss; the elderly Chinese men singing a mix of Sinatra and Asian classics often fell into the "miss" category, while the live jazz was often a "hit." About ten years ago, a dance club called Firecracker brought a cool mix of urban music lovers to this formerly dull spot on the first and third Friday of each month, and though it ended its long run in 2009, Firecracker put the place on the map club-wise. If you're reading this book, you probably don't really care about the clubby aspect as much as the room itself, but it bears noting that some really slammin' parties still go down here regularly (Full Frontal, a flamboyant disco bacchanal and Boombox, an old school hip-hop groover).

Now for the divey deets: duct taped-up seating, greasy cracked walls, rickety restrooms, year-round Christmas lights, a strange odor that seems to permeate both upstairs and downstairs, and drinks in plastic cups only (you risk harsh reprimand if you try to sip on the flashy dance floor). Despite the rundown interior, Grand Star is much beloved, both for its disco decadence and its open to all vibe. Unlike Hop Louie, the staff here is quite amiable, and you can often find the Quon brothers Wally and Frank hanging out at the bar or boogieing at the clubs. Someone even made a documentary about the place and its regulars called "One Night At The Grand Star" which was run as part of PBS' "Independent Lens" series several years ago. Though its DJ-driven dance bashes have outshined the space itself in recent years, Grand Star's old world appeal and Chinatown alley location are why many young clubber types check out events here in the first place. It's continually cited as an alternative to Hollywood's nightlife frenzy, which ensures interest from new promoters looking to give their parties indie cred.

Hop Louie

950 Mei Ling Way
Phone: (213) 628-4244

Dive Bar Rating

In the summer of 1938, Chinatown's Central Plaza was dedicated in a gala Grand Opening ceremony. "New" Chinatown (as opposed to the old one, from the 1800s which was more of an industrial/residential area, located where Union Station now stands) is still one of LA's liveliest tourist attractions. Even for those of us who grew up here, C-Town's colorful lantern-layered entrances, kitschy curio shops, and coin-specked fountain and wishing well provided a somewhat exotic mini-escape from the norms of La-La life. Enjoying an authentic Chinese dinner in one of the family style restaurants (love the ones with the lazy-susans in the middle of the tables) became a regular excursion of mine during the late eighties, and later on, in the mid-nineties, when the area saw a new slew of art galleries and funky shops open up. Too bad a traumatic experience involving night-crawlers (real ones, not club-hoppers) at one eatery a few years ago made me swear off dining in the area ever again.

Though it's under an ornate, photo-op-worthy pagoda just steps away from my beloved wishing well, I can't say I had ever attempted to chomp at Hop Louie, even before the creepy-crawly incident, mostly because the general consensus on the greasy grub (served upstairs) from pals who had eaten it was "beware." Louie does get some love, at least by locals, for its ornate downstairs bar, a small room known for cheap, strong cocktails and infamously gruff, old bartenders. Actually, gruff might be putting it mildly: a couple of 'em seem to relish being downright rude. For LA's braver bar-hoppers, however, this is part of Louie's allure. There's also a jukebox filled with requisite classic rock and soul, and a few drinks made to slay like "the Scorpion" "Singapore Sling" and Mai Tai's (the prices vary depending on the bartender's mood, which as previously stated, isn't usually very chipper). However, the main reason to go to HL is the room itself, which seems to be almost untouched décor-wise since it was erected in 1941. It would seem that Mr. Louie (yes, there really was a Hop Louie and in the '60s, he also owned a slew of tiki-themed restaurants) didn't do much to update the place when he took it over and renamed it (it was originally called The Golden Pagoda) in the '80s. From its dusty fixtures to its rusty restrooms to its crusty staff, this one always feels like a hop back in time.

Back Door Pub

813 S. Flower Street
Phone: (213) 627-6981

Dive Bar Rating

For years, I had been hearing about the Back Door from friends who lived and worked in the Downtown area. They loved its hidden location (it's in the back of a hotel and you have to enter through a crud and mud covered alleyway) and its cheap, super-strong drinks. Unfortunately, each time I tried to go, the place was closed. One time, I got there too late (it closes at nine); on another occasion, I stopped by on a Saturday evening, not realizing that the place hasn't been open on Saturdays for decades; and still another time it was just after the holidays and the bar was closed for a week.

Let's just say by the time I finally was able to step foot inside, *I really needed a drink*. And the Back Door did not disappoint. There's only one gal manning the show, a sweet lass by the name of Kimberly, and not only does she pour one strong cocktail, she'll fix it if it's not one hundred percent what you were hoping for. I went old school (well my old school, as in my drink of choice from back in '94, a Midori Sour) and Kimberly kept adding the liqueur until the drink was the perfect shade of Day-Glo green. Not many dive 'tenders would do that, and there are not many dive 'tenders that I would dare ask to do that. Hell, there are not that many dives that I'd actually order that kind of wussy drink in, period. But the relaxed feel of the Back Door, which is rarely crowded after the day crowd leaves around seven (which is why they close so early) makes you feel like anything is okay, with the exception of getting belligerent, of course. Despite the warm and fuzzy atmosphere, Kim is still one tough cookie, and she's been known to throw out cracky cretins and snarky snakes that slither in from the alley.

While an old guy who worked at the bar for decades before Kim —and may or may not have been ripping off the place—apparently hated cleaning (pals who used to go there described the bar as filthy), the room, which has shiny black and red booths, bright walls and deco style art posters, is pretty spanking these days. It's also very comfy and serene. There's only one old clunker of a TV set, and it never has sports on. Instead, Kim keeps it on a nifty, '80's new wave heavy cable music channel. Drink prices run in the $6-$8 range, but like I said, they're strong. And, if you overdo it, you've got a hotel to stay in just a few stumbles away. Take note of the Back Door's actual hours: Tuesday through Friday, from noon-8 p.m.

Bar 107

107 4th St.
Phone: (213) 625-7382

Dive Bar Rating

Everything but the kitchen sink (on crack) would be an apt description of the décor of this junky, high-ceilinged downtown circus. A snapshot tally of the wacky interior—which makes *Sanford and Son* seem minimalist—includes: a leg lamp, mounted buck heads in trucker hats, a jackalope, a barber pole, piñatas, framed pics of Don Rickles and (coincidence?) Redd Foxx, retro toys, the obligatory velvet paintings and a life-size Indian statue that greets you—and bids you buh-bye—at the door. New stuff also seems to appear every month or so. "Was that piñata there the last time I came," you'll find yourself asking, and however pissed drunk you may have been, it probably wasn't.

While the kitschy clutter might be unrivaled in bar land (Cha Cha Lounge, which is not in this book, comes close, though it's not as haphazard or dirty feeling), 107 is ultimately more about the odd moments to be had inside (and out), than about the oddities hanging from the ceiling: homeless men doing Michael Jackson moves; dogs barking and pooping (the place is mutt-friendly); rockabilly chicks pouting in the old school b&w photo booth; and tatted-up loft dwellers hard-pounding the tallboys ($5 PBRs, Millers, and Tekates) and building up the unfortunate courage for crooning bad '80s anthems (Toto, Billy Ocean) or bustin' a move (badly) in the adjacent dance room. "Gong Show Karaoke," hosted by a dude named Bong Jovi every Wednesday gets pretty wild, and parties with self-consciously retro names like "Leisure Suite" and "Ghetto Blaster" attract bodies from all over the city. Of course, that means that the inevitable douche factor has infiltrated the bar somewhat, making the locals none too happy. Still, the bar has an innate 'tude (and badass security) that never allow things to get too bad. Come in the middle of the week, on a non-club night, for the real deal freak and fiend show, with a larger smattering of the latter. (I wasn't kidding about the crack in my intro; you'll often encounter those with a penchant for the pipe walking in). Currently, 107 shares the block with a bunch of hip, arty fashion stores and once a month a popular "Artwalk" event brings eccentrics and tastemakers alike to the area, with most everyone congregating here after the festivities. Look for the "Heileman's Old Style"/"Ollie's Live Bait and Tackle" sign out front.

Five Stars Bar

269 S Main St.
Phone: (213) 625-1037

The residential and recreational renaissance of Downtown LA has been in the works for several years now, and as of this writing, it's safe to say that we're still smack dab in the middle of the transition. This means that pricey lofts owned by actors and trust fund brats still overlook dirty streets and their associated mix of the homeless, addicts, and the occasional lady/gent of the evening. It also means that you'll encounter velvet ropes just as impenetrable as those seen in Hollywood right after you've been bombarded by panhandlers.

Despite the slow march toward respectability, the dilapidated downtown dens that haven't yet been touched by urban renewal retain a certain cache and mystery. With towering ceilings, dingy yet elaborate tiled flooring and hidden crevices galore, the Five Stars Bar is one of the area's most spacious multi-purpose rooms. The kindly chica—many of the patrons are of Mexican descent—behind the bar is very obliging, and it isn't hard to talk her into a tour of the cavernous multi-leveled spot's unseen areas. The back and upstairs of this old building have a Scooby Doo cartoon like quality: dark, cobwebbed, and filled with old furniture and props that would make a great haunted house on Halloween. Most of the action takes place downstairs in the main room, though, which is actually fairly clean and bright, and zestfully covered with paintings and photography from local artists. Underground dance parties, post Art Walk soirees, bands, DJs and whatnot take over Five Stars on a regular basis, though most nights its a listless mix of *abuelitos* (grandpas) glued to the tube and random bar hoppers making their way through for a cheap starter chug before moving on to livelier locales.

Hank's

840 S Grand Ave.
Phone: (213) 623-7718

Dive Bar Rating

I can't start a write-up of this old watering hole without first mentioning its namesake, Mr. Hank Holzer, a former boxer who opened the place in 1954 and was known to hold court nightly, downing screwdrivers with pals such as former LA mayor Richard Riordan. Though Holzer died in 1997, newspaper clippings and ill-placed knick-knacks still offer a visual narrative history to this cozy, wood accented old fave and its former owner. These days, however, a big part of Hank's mystique comes from its locale: the ground floor of a bizarre little downtown hotel known as The Stillwell, which opened in 1912. Like the bar itself, the hotel feels like something out of a noir crime novel. Quiet and seemingly quaint (compared with the newer spots in the area), there's a hint of the ominous here, and you get the feeling some shady wheeling and dealing probably went down in both the ragged leather booths of the bar and the box-like rooms of the hotel back in the day.

If you drink a lot at Hank's, you pretty much can't avoid the Stillwell since it shares the same bathroom (if not for a potty break I might have never explored the maze-like layout which includes both an Indian and Mexican restaurant in the back of the building). And while Hank's similarly cavernous design includes a long walkway to its rear and crevices where one could easily engage in some bad behavior without anyone in the front bar being any the wiser, the crowd who goes here are generally good eggs, hence the chill, homey ambiance. Chomping on too much of the complimentary over-salted popcorn or sampling one too many drink specials seems as depraved as things get nowadays.

King Eddy Saloon

131 W 5th St.
Phone: (213) 629-2023

Hailed as the oldest bar in downtown, the 120-year old King is known as much for its former regulars (literary figures, crime leaders) as it is for its current, shall we say colorful, crowd. John Fante and Charles Bukowski were both frequent flyers at this Skid Row-adjacent bar, which has managed to survive from prohibition (it had a downstairs speakeasy during LA's dry period, which the local police allegedly left alone in exchange for payoffs) to the recent recession, which has probably helped the place flourish, since they make the cheapest vodka cranberry in this whole book ($3).

The raw, somewhat ravaged room, which is on the ground floor The King Edward Hotel, is a must see for history buffs: the bar is such a liquor landmark that it's included as a stop on the historic "Esotouric Bus Tours" and has been featured on the History Channel's "Cities of the Underworld." However, even without its intriguing past, its present still makes it a required, if seemingly cracky/wacky, drinking destination. While the fact that the bar doesn't discriminate against the local druggies gives it a whiff of danger, the overall vibe is still welcoming and comfy in spite of the unsavory elements, of which there are quite a few, including, in no particular order: the omnipresent dude at the door asking if he can trade you four quarters for a dollar bill (took me a while to figure that one out, but for those who you can't, its how they "roll" in this part of town); the toothless quotient; the spaced-out, non-sequitur conversations and comments heard above the jukebox's blast of soul, blues, and rock classics; the rotund (working?) gals in unflatteringly tight getups gyrating at said jukebox; and the layered aroma of chemical cleaners, cigarette smoke (there's a cage-like "smoking section" to the left of the room), urine and B.O. This place is so chock full of dive clichés, it's comical and sad at the same time.

La Cita Bar

366 S. Hill St.
Phone: (213) 687-7111

Dive Bar Rating

Makeovers are of course, nothing new in Los Angeles nightlife, but at least the guys who bought this downtown Mexican ranchero room (which includes some of the same heads behind both the Short Stop and Footsies buyouts) have attempted to keep the place's tacky Tijuana bar-like environs intact. A red and green Christmas lit ceiling, crimson leather and brass accents, exposed brick walls, cobblestone flooring, and a very strange, very small stage overlooking the dance floor make La Cita a sleazetastic backdrop for both a new cluster of hedonistic happenings and the Spanish-music fiestas that have had amigos flocking here for decades.

Despite its popular club promotions at night, La Cita by day is the same Mexican manor it always has been. The Latino regulars still spend their afternoons (and mornings, as the bar opens at 10 a.m.) sipping Bud Lights and tequila shots while watching soccer or horse racing on the TV. Sundays, called Hacienda Nights, feature live salsa and Latin music. The fly-for-white guy groups who boogie to disco and ghetto-tech beats at Thursday's Dance Right (which often features famed artist Shepard Fairey on the decks) and Friday's Punky Reggae, an irie/hardcore clash, probably have no idea just how authentic this place remains when they're not there. If you want a taste of both worlds, the ample outdoor area is a good bet, especially on weekend afternoons. And, the libations out there are stronger and cheaper. For drinking *and* dancing, my favorite evening promotion at La Cita is Mustache Mondays, a gay, Latin-friendly grind-a-thon that makes best use of the place's low brow bodaciousness. The aforementioned stage, complete with sticker covered railing, was probably built for mariachis, but when drag queens, tighty-whitey-wearing go-go boys, and assorted freaks trample the thing, its potential as an entertainment showcase reaches new heights.

Redwood Bar

316 W. 2nd St.
Phone: (213) 680-2600

The original Redwood, which opened in 1943 and relocated to 2nd Street, just west of downtown's famed green-hued tunnel in 1970, always attracted ancient boozers and nightlife buccaneers, so when new owners Christian Frizzell and Dev Dugal took it over three years ago and made it into a pirate themed bar, it didn't feel like too much of an incursion. To say that the Redwood's refurbishment was well received at all is really saying something because this old spot, though musty and dusty before the alterations, was beloved both for its history (JFK, Richard Nixon, and gangster Mickey Cohen are all said to have sipped here while in town—though not together) and its well-kept secret feel. It was like the bar that time forgot, and for several years, it was almost exclusively a hangout for journalists from the nearby headquarters of the *L.A. Times*.

The new interior, thankfully, avoids anything too Jack Sparrowesque. There are well-placed skulls leering about and old ship paintings and some corner nets, and the tables are barrel tops, but everything is kind of muted and old looking. The main accents here are on wood and brass, and though the place is clean, you still get a sense of timelessness upon walking in. This is truly a drinking den to get jolly in (try the rum drinks and the yummy bar food, served all night), even more so when live music takes over the tiny stage in the rear of the room a few nights a week. The entertainment features some of the most adventurous acts from L.A. and beyond rocking the ship. One such act, the infamous songwriter/roc Svengali Kim Fowley, is known to bring his "Sexual Underground" variety shows to the bar on a regular basis. Check out the wonderfully woozy blues ode he wrote just for the Redwood on the bar's website.

Tony's Saloon

2017 E 7th St.
Phone: (213) 622-5523

Dive Bar Rating

"Downtown bars are the antitheses of Hollywood bars right now," muses Cedd Moses, a man who many consider the bar czar of Los Angeles. "Downtown bars are all about great drinks, friendly charismatic people and spots with history and depth." Moses should know. His company, 213 Downtown, has helmed the reinvention of some of the area's most legendary old drinking holes, including the snazzy and jazzy Broadway Bar, the whiskey worshipping Seven Grand, and old movie-star-ish glam gem Golden Gopher. "A dive bar has soul, characters and a tinge of debauchery,' he explains. "Our bars were in great historic buildings and had plenty of soul already. We just had to bring out their inherent character."

Many of Moses' restored relics, which happen to be some of my favorite bars in LA, retain a dive-ish essence, but I couldn't in good conscience include them in this book, if only because they are just too damn gorgeous. However, his latest acquisition, Tony's Saloon, is an exception. Like the other bars, it's quite handsome, but its "inherent character" is more prevalent than in the others. Tony's stands in a rather remote part of downtown, and the truth is, fraidy cats like me wouldn't dare drive there if the place didn't have its own parking lot. Inside, the room is relaxed yet unfussy, sparse, yet eye-catching, especially the large rich wood back bar, which Moses doesn't even take credit for; it was brought over from a nineteenth century saloon in Utah by previous owners. "We just needed to restore some integrity to the rest of the room. It wasn't comfortable," Moses explains. Comfy new touches include booths, soft lamp lighting, and a great smoking patio complete with a ping-pong table. There are also noticeable nods to Hunter S Thompson throughout. Moses says that the bar reminded him of Thompson's famed haunt the Woody Creek Tavern in Colorado, so he "decided to honor one of our great American writers and boozers." Of course that includes an abundance of H.S.T.'s favorite bourbons behind the bar. The liquor selection—like all of Moses' dens—is mind blowing, and not surprisingly there's something about his place that brings out one's inner literary lush.

I've felt pretentious pulling out the pen and notepad in some bars, but not here. The long-standing muse-like relationship between scribes and the spots where they imbibe has been referenced before, but Tony's might be the first LA barfly hive to go beyond the usual Bukowski buzz.

M House

1263 W Temple St.
Phone: (213) 482-3828

Dive Bar Rating

You might ask yourself, "Am I at a bar, a restaurant, or an Asian family's living room?" when you enter this very strange food and liquor joint, best known for its on-the-downlow drunken after hours events. Avocado green couches, grandma-ish, eighties-style neo-modern home fixtures, and a huge painting of the proprietress ("M") behind the area where occasional jazz bands play make for an odd setting that just gets odder as the night goes on (and sometimes that's 'til the crack of dawn). This domicile-like den, also known as "Dinner House M" has somewhat fallen victim to the Eastside hip parade, providing the ultimate ironic habitat for parties as diverse as that of Radiohead's Thom Yorke post-show shindig and a weekly gay-heavy gathering from the always ahead of the trends Mustache Mondays boys (see La Cita Bar) who rage "until they kick us out." Sometimes, there's a $6 cover charge, which you won't mind paying after 2 a.m. when things are slammin' underground style, but can be less than worth it when no one is in the place, which is common during normal hours. If the place is empty and there's no promotion or live music that night, you can console yourself with the Anime-ish eye candy behind the bar pouring drinks, in particular, a cute pun-kette in bows and funky makeup and an Asian metalhead dude always dressed head-to-toe in studs, boots and leather ensembles, ala Poison and Ratt. While the servers may be friendly, the drink prices—especially for this sketchy a neighborhood—ain't, and be aware that if you walk in looking glam rather than grunge, you'll probably be gouged accordingly.

Silver Platter

2700 W 7th St
No Phone

You'll see a fair share of Latin trannies and queens at the Silver Platter, and they are, in this Latina's opinion, the most caliente of the cross-dressing/transgendered nationalities. There are exceptions of course, but Caucasians in dress or transition still tend to look like dudes most of the time; think Tootsie, John Travolta, even Divine. Anyway, the Platter has been a hospitable environment for multy-culty sexual self-expression since it first opened in 1963. Back then, and in the decades that followed, Rogelio Ramirez welcomed mostly cowboy hatted Mexican gays, and the soundtrack followed suit, ranchero, salsa, some disco. When his brother Gonzalo took over in the '90s, a shift occurred, and a notable increase in trans women made the platter chatter anew. Still, the place wasn't even on the map with most LA dive-hoppers (even gay ones) until 2008, when the popular Tuesday night party Wildness amped up the hair mousse quotient.

You tend to hear the word "ghetto" attached to the Platter more so than with other homo/trans haunts, and that's got as much to do with its location adjacent to MacArthur Park (a known druggie connection spot) and its tacky interior—a tiny dance area, black and white checkered floor, a sparkly curtain for a performance backdrop, requisite disco ball, and flashing lights—as it does the political subtext behind the partying that goes down here. In a way, keeping the Platter "ghetto," however derogatory the term might be interpreted by some, means it will never get too mainstream or too straight-laced. Maintaining the place's history is important to those who love the Platter, and a new documentary, entitled Damelo Todo, filmed from the perspective of the immigrant, queer patrons of the bar, should insure that no matter what changes occur in the area, Silver Platter's past won't be forgotten. It may not be everyone's shot of tequila, but Silver has a sincerity and creative zest not seen at many other bars. Some might find it ironic that one of the most "real" bars in LA is filled a lot of chicas who aren't exactly one hundred percent real themselves, but this humble yet happy place is a mess of contradictions that comes together and just works (it).

ECHO PARK

Gold Room

1558 W Sunset Blvd.
Phone: (213) 482-5259

This quintessential Echo Park dive is wobbling down a not so straight line between gentrified grooverville and Espanol-only stalwart, which isn't as adversarial as it might seem. The Gold Room is an exercise in polarity, especially on weekends, when shaggy heads sit at the bar next to greased up old timers (and baseball capped Dodgers fans during game season; the Stadium is up the street after all). The jukebox is turned off and a DJ offers schizo mixes from a laptop in a dark corner, sonically hopping back and forth in an attempt to please the very mixed crowd: tejano, then rock, salsa, then hip-hop, reggaeton into pop. The Gold Room has been touted for its voluptuous barmaids, but there's always a cool older gent pouring generously behind the bar as well; sometimes its even the owner, Pepe, who hangs out often with his amigos, surely marveling at the bar's new wave of fans.

The slender room, like the crowd and the music, is a mish-mash: a mirrored bar shrine with etched tropical logo, a space-themed ceiling complete with planetary mural, cushiony restaurant style booths across from the bar (they got new ones that match the room in January of 2010) . Those booths are hot property for the newbie set, many of whom come for what may be the bar's biggest draw for both struggling heads de la *familia* and starving band dudes alike: free tacos (in addition to bottomless bowls of peanuts on the counters and tables). While most stand and chomp while balancing their piled-high grease-limp paper plates *and* drinks, the smart scoffers get there early or wait patiently for one of the tiny booths that line the right side wall. Scoring a seat at the Gold Room to devour your tacos and cerveza in comfort is akin to hitting the jackpot.

Little Joy

1477 Sunset Blvd.
Phone: (213) 250-3417

What makes a dive too hip? Whatever it is, the writing's on the wall at Little Joy—literally. The gutter-ish grotto (formerly a gay amigo au-go-go) is swathed with graffiti everywhere you look inside, but not with the gang tags you're likely to see on the streets just outside (surprising considering it's in the heart of Echo Park, a.k.a Echo Parque, and you if you have no idea what I'm talking about, rent Allison Anders' *Mi Vida Loca*). Even the local cholos seem to be scared off by this shabby shack, which mostly attracts hobo-ish Charles Manson looking chaps and the thift store garbed femmes who live to follow n' flirt 'with 'em.

Little Joy remains a hotspot even if it seems as though the new owners don't know what to do with it. An exterior mural was painted only to be removed months later, but the major makeover's mainstays did include slightly less putrid bathrooms (Joy was famous for its stinky, leaky johns), a bigger—if pricier—liquor selection, more mainstream-minded DJs, and an interior paint job. Which brings us back to the graffiti. Regulars might have been appalled when the spot's signature Sharpie'd walls got covered-up in late '08, but it seems as if the cool kids are just as persistent as the gang taggers, and it was just a matter of days til the ballpoint and marker'd masterpieces returned. You could literally spend hours reading the walls here, and while it might mostly be a mix of bad art school sketches, pretentious poetry, and miscellaneous non-sensical bullshit, the stuff gets more and more interesting, profound even, with each drink you down. I knew I had too many (stiff) vodka crans the last time I was there when the rules for joining some dude's cult started to seem really deep and existential: 1) turnips are mandatory for breakfast; 2) no chewing gum; 3) all members must kill at least one wolverine; 4) light's off after 10 p.m.; 5) showering is optional; 6) kool-aid must be drunk at all thymes (his spelling, not mine). The above may or may not be covered up by the time you read this, but rest assured something just as ridiculous will have taken its place.

The lighting here used to be mercifully low, which may have

made the walls harder to read, but did make for a shadier, groovier atmosphere. The unflattering florescent tint it's got now makes it feel like a garage or basement (of your crazy next door neighbor). There's two pool tables, which always look like they're about to collapse, but haven't (yet), and the seating is a mash of torn and taped booths and hard metal patio chairs—the kind that give girls in short skirts waffle-printed thighs, so bringing a sweater and sitting on it is a good idea. Better yet, don't wear a short skirt when you go here.

No matter how hip this area has become, it can still be a dangerous stroll. Pals of mine have been mugged walking down to the bar (and the Short Stop a block down). Though Little Joy used to be a good place to score miscellaneous intoxicants, we hear that element subsided with the mini-makeover. For this reason, and due to the drink price increase and the fact that a band named itself after the place (moreover, a band that includes a member of The Strokes who also happened to date Drew Barrymore at one point), we must deduct two dive points from Little Joy's otherwise high dive rating.

The Short Stop

1455 W Sunset Blvd.
Phone: (213) 482-4942

Dive Bar Rating

Proximity to Dodger Stadium inspired the name, but this Echo Park homer's reputation (which its current clientele are surely clueless about) came from the (bad) boys in blue: the LAPD. The place was a hangout for corrupt officers involved in the Rampart division scandal, in which more than seventy officers from the nearby station were implicated in misconduct, some involving payoffs from none other than Death Row Records' Marion "Suge" Knight. After that, the beloved "cop bar" as many called it, saw a significant drop-off in badged regulars, forcing its original owner to sell.

In came four friends and investors from the entertainment industry, including former Afghan Whigs frontman Greg Dulli, Oliver Wilson, Charles Gaiennie, and Dave Neupert, who not only breathed new life into the spot by getting their numerous friends and fans to flock there (beginning with a grand-reopening party on New Years Eve of 2001) but also managed to strike a relaxed balance between nightclub and nostalgic dive. Unlike other revamped bars at the time, the new Short Stoppers kept its name (though it did lose the old sign out front) and most of its décor. The new owners brought in some of the city's best DJs to the adjacent dance room, and since then, the red-hued floor has become one of the ultimate Echo Park/Silver Lake "It" spots—a mess of ironic tees and skinny dungarees, white boy fros and purpled polished toes. On weekends and hot DJ nights (Wednesdays and Thursdays) there is literally a line down the block by 10:30 or so to get into the place, and though long-time doorman Justice is a cool dude, the usual flirty femmes and I-know-so-and-so braggadashery will not shorten the wait time.

Once inside, prepare to wait some more for your drinks, which I've found to be pretty potent if not terribly cheap ($7-$8) upon most visits. Because of the strength of the drinks, I inevitably end up on the dance floor, shaking like a fool with some convulsing *Napoleon Dynamite* look-a-like to Young MC remixes (the floor here is always fullest when the soundtrack is early nineties dance hits and hip-hop). I usually gravitate toward the nerdy types, but unfortunately for us ladies, the Stop's dancing area often seems to have its share of more aggressive (i.e., too touchy-feely) grinders. Pumping it up with a posse if you're a gal is a good idea.

Though the scammers and jammers can be annoying, the good stuff here cancels out anything bad. There's a great pool table area, a black & white photo booth that's extra brightly lit and thereby makes everyone look good, and a guy usually selling $1 tamales near the door. In some ways, the Short Stop might be a scenester circus, but Neupert and Co. aim to keep the inner dive alive, which means there are still many reminders of the cop bar days: memorabilia like billyclub parts, badges, patches and gun lockers, and a bounty of bullet holes behind the bar and in the front door.

Hipster Havens

The Bar

The Bigfoot Lodge

Burgundy Room

The Short Stop

Little Joy

Footsies

Little Cave

Silver Lake Lounge

SILVER LAKE/ATWATER

Akbar

4356 Sunset Blvd.
Phone: (323) 665-6810

Dive Bar Rating

From its low-budget Moroccan hideaway look, to its jammin' juke-box and DJs, to the madcap mix of patrons (it varies with the night, but a good estimate of preferences is about 60 percent gay, 20 percent straight, and 20 percent ambivalent), Akbar continues to be a fave with open-minded guzzlers and nuzzlers alike. Opened in 1996 by Scott Craig and Peter Alexander, the idea behind this dark, kitschy spot was a neighborhood bar minus the locals-only 'tude. Silver Lake may be tres-trendy, and was since long before this place opened, but you never feel like an interloper at Akbar, no matter where you're from or whom you like to kiss. Indeed, this bar's buoyant brew of art-fully attired boys and gals, rocker chicks and dudes, bears, femmes, queens, pierced and plain bods, and everything in between, has made it the best "mixed" scene around, recognized as such by every local rag in town. The owners added an adjacent dance room next door a few years ago, and the decksmiths always work the crowd into a spas-tic frenzy, usually for free. If you don't like to get wet (from sweat) or inhale B.O. (boy odors), though, the main bar might be more your speed. The drinks are tasty and dirt-cheap, and the above-mentioned jukebox has something for everyone, from the Sex Pistols and the Ramones to George Michael and Nina Simone. The bathrooms can be somewhat scary, especially if you pop in late in the evening as my pals and I are prone to do, but lucky for us ladies, our loo usually lacks the tempestuous tangle seen in front of the fellas' (and surely inside too). I'm not alone in choosing Akbar as a night "closer." The last pit stop before heading home and crashing can be pivotal in how one surveys an overall nightlife experience. This unassuming yet high-spirited spot leaves one with a generally good feeling, and no matter how much damage their brain-numbing drinks may inflict, it always seems worth it the next morning.

Le Barcito

3909 W Sunset Blvd.
Phone: (323) 644-3515

Dive Bar Rating

While Barcito is a place where boys in cha-cha heels like to party, it's also an historical landmark—#939 in the City of Los Angeles' Historic Cultural Monument List. It was known as The Black Cat Tavern in the '60s, and an incident that occurred inside the bar on New Years Eve 1967, was a spark for the gay rights movement in LA. That evening, the place was raided and six men were charged with lewd conduct for simply kissing at midnight, while sixteen additional patrons were taken in just for congregating at the bar. Allegedly, barstaff were also beaten by the police. In protest, one of the first gay pride demonstrations ever in the United States (pre-dating New York City's Stonewall riots by two years) was held just outside the front door, prompting gays in Los Angeles to mobilize like never before. One of the founders of the respected gay mag the Advocate happened to be one of those arrested that fateful eve, and he credits that experience as the inspiration for creating the publication. Since then, the purple-paint covered Tijuana-bar style drinking and dancing spot (walk in and the colorful patrons almost blend in thanks to chaotic video screens, flashing lights and smoke machines) has served as host to other activist assemblages, most recently in protest to Proposition 8 (the antigay marriage prop). The more things change the more they stay the same, unfortunately.

As for the obvious changes, the structure that used to comprise the Black Cat is now part laundermat (which has closed as of this book's printing; what replaces it is anyone's guess). The street itself is right in the heart of the Sunset Junction, where in the past few years an Intelligentsia coffee house and a few pricey boutiques have changed the complexion of the neighborhood from gay and Hispanic to straight, white and scenester-ish. Still, despite what S'Lake naysayers might suggest, the community's flamboyant, multy-culty mix hasn't been completely obliterated. As long as seasoned Silver Lake posts like Barcito remain, it's not likely to either.

The Eagle

4219 Santa Monica Blvd.
Phone: (323) 669-9472

Dive Bar Rating

First and foremost, let me state something proudly: I am a full-on fag-hag. (And yeah, I can use the F word. I got approval from my gay boyfriends okay?) But even the most fervent of Queer Dears/ Fruit Flies/Flame Dames/Homo Honeys can be made to feel less than welcome in certain gay bars. It's just the way it is sometimes, especially as the evening nears last call. The ever-astute Margaret Cho (a notorious hag) calls this bewitching hour of boy-dom—when us real girls become superfluous—"dick o'clock," but at some bars its testosterone time all the time. For the most part, the Eagle is one these bars. Touting itself as "LA's premiere leather bar" this dark dungeon-like drinking and dancing hub doesn't see a lot of queens or flamboyant femmes or real gals. It's more a forest o' fellas: bears (aka big hairy dudes), 'stached biker types, and muscley men in assless chaps. With party promotions monikered "Throbbing Thursdays," "Meatrack" and "Wheel of Torture" this spot is not for the faint of heart, gay or not. Weak noses (there's an ever-present pungent aroma best described as crotchy—a blend of urine, pelvic sweat and who knows what else) and prude patrons (gay porn is often shown on screens inside the main bar area, there's usually lube available in the bathrooms and floors are often sticky) need not land here, nor should snobbier WeHo homos. The cash-only drinks are served in plastic cups and they are hit or miss depending on the 'tender (it seems the bigger and scarier the server, the bigger and scarier the sips). Even for an experienced gay barhopper like moi, a visit to the Eagle can be somewhat intimidating, though for the most part, everyone's pretty amiable here… it is Silver Lake after all. Straight and poly-sexual parties will want to flock to the expansive outdoor patio, which provides a bit of an escape from the muggy/manly mayhem inside and seems more about boozing than cruising.

Hyperion Tavern

1941 Hyperion Ave.
Phone: (323) 665-1941

Way before it became a pop culture sensation, this little Silver Lake beer shack garnered national attention for its weekly Guitar Hero nights. However, while music mags like *Rolling Stone* may have focused on the faux riffing going on here, the local press (including yours truly) were far more intrigued by another kind of fingering that went on in the space, though prior to its current guise. You see, the Tavern is housed in the space formerly known as Cuffs, Silver Lake's legendary, hardest (pun intended) hardcore leather bar, a spot where man-on-man sexscapades and boys in bondage were among the tamer of amusements (Apparently there are still "glory holes" to be found in the walls here, though I've never seen them). As a Silver Lake local, I often walked by the tiny wood planked hut of heaving homo-lust as a teen, and wondered what wildness was going on inside. When the place shut down and reopened as Hyp Tav, its salacious and secretive past was one of its selling points, as the masses finally got a glimpse inside one of the city's most infamous hedonist huts, scrubbed clean, but not too clean.

Eventually, this bar with no sign outside (there is a barber pole instead), limited libations (beer, but no wine and, if they happen to have it that night, ale) and a peculiar new look (law books cover one wall, a monstrous chandelier hangs from the ceiling and the wood bar stands in an awkward spot that's not quite flush with the front wall) established its own quirky identity. While the Guitar Hero (updated to Rock Band) nights became staples, another weekly gathering known as Club Ding A Ling soon drew its own share of attention for bringing in an inspired mix of bizarre, performance art like bands: trannies in wheelchairs, Charles Manson worshipers, robotic noise makers, and occasionally, bonafide rockstars on the slum. Don Bolles of the legendary punk band The Germs is one of the DJs and a frequent master of ceremonies for the sonic insanity, which like most nights here, is free. Another off-kilter theme night is "Give UP!" the Dublab DJ collective's evening of sad and woeful sounds. Bring cash (there's no ATM) and dress lightly; even in the winter this place is a sauna, which may have added to the atmosphere at Cuffs, but not here. This little bar may be a lot of things, but a meat market is not one of them.

The Red Lion

2366 Glendale Blvd.
Phone: (323) 662-5337

Dive Bar Rating

The Red Lion's quaint, old world German décor, cutesy dirndl-costumed bar maidens and heavy, meaty menu leaves an impression that is both mental and physical, especially when you waddle out of the place with a belly bloated with beer, sausage, and sauerkraut. The homely, slightly shoddy downstairs bar offers a dizzying array of brews (Spaten Lager, Warsteiner pilsner, Bitburger and Erdinger Hefeweizen to name but a few), which, for only a few dollars more than the standard pint-size glass, you can have served in a stein. However, when my friends and I first frequented the Lion several years ago, you could get your beer in a giant glass boot, which was big enough for two, even three medium sized gals to grab a buzz off of. When I requested a beer boot upon a recent visit, I was informed the bar was "out of" 'em. This was strange, since I didn't remember them being souvenir "take-home" glasses? A few weeks later, I put in a call to the bar about the boot glasses, and a staffer told me, rudely I might add, that they would be getting them again, *someday*, but she couldn't say when. She also added that they break too easily, in her opinion, which kind of explains it all I guess. While the steins they offer instead of the boots these days are big, they sadly do not match the ornate German novelties on display atop the bar.

Opened in 1960, the Lion actually started off as an English pub with darts and the whole nine yards. It established its German theme in 1963, and saw a slight remodel (including the popular outdoor beer garden area) about ten years ago. There's a really festive yet chill beer garden, which features cozy dark green leather booths and a middle-aged organist who plays an utterly astounding mix of tunes, from umlaut favorites like The Scorpions and Motley Crue to song-stresses like Cyndi Lauper and Madonna to prog-gods Foreigner and Journey (he even takes requests). On the second Thursday of the month, a campy crooner impersonating beloved German *Volksmusik* singer Heino meanders throughout the tiny bar in a blonde wig and dark shades singing ironic versions of songs like "Superfreak."

Tips: get the brackwurst not the knackwurst, expect to wait if you dine in the main level bar (the staff may be cute, but they ain't quick) and if you don't have good parking car-ma, don't even try to squeeze into the steep, cramped lot. And finally, take a cab home if you're messed-up, not like the jerk who totaled my Nissan Sentra after having "dinner" here in 2007. The dubious old dude blamed me for a collision that happened only a few blocks from the bar, but after he revealed he was coming from the Red Lion in his deposition, his insurance company quickly settled the case. Achtung baby!

Silver Lake Lounge

2906 W Sunset Blvd.
Phone: (323) 663-9636

Dive Bar Rating

While this smallish rock music cave might be most well known as a live music venue for the too-cool-to-shampoo set, it's still first and foremost a dive bar. It's cash only (there's an ATM machine, natch), the bartenders are middle aged Latino gents, and older alkies can be found here on any given evening pretty much oblivious to the frizzy/dizzy hipsteratti that come for the bands. On weekends, it's strictly Latin trannies and queens, who provide an awesome dress up spectacle and stage show for likeminded and trendy locals alike.

Since 1997, Scott Sterling, one of the guys largely responsible for Silver Lake's current rep as a music Mecca, has been transforming the Lounge into "The Fold," and the crowds and the room make for a combustible combo. The bonanza of beards, faded t-shirts, boys in girls jeans, and waify chicks who appear to have gotten dressed in the dark and combed their hair with dinner forks are indicative of Silver Lake's sometimes silly aesthetic, but fashion faux pas or not, there's nothing silly about the sheer amount of talent that has emerged from the area and particularly, this narrow, beat-up coal-mine black room. Some of the artists who've played here (under the carnival-like "salvation" sign Sterling claims to have fished out of Lake Michigan) include Beck, Vampire Weekend, Cold War Kids, The Bird & The Bee, Black Rebel Motorcycle Club, Devendra Banhart, The Kills, And You Will Know Us By The Trail Of The Dead, and the Silversun Pickups, named for the liquor store across the street. Sterling has offered music at other venues around town, but none has ever been able to match the consistency he's had at this shabby corner of Silver Lake and Sunset. Ironically, he's said to have chosen the name "The Fold" because after a few shows, that's exactly what he expected it to do. It didn't turn out like that, of course, and these days the name is about bringing people into the Silver Lake music fold, bad boho garb optional.

Smog Cutter

864 N Virgil Ave.
Phone: (323) 660-4626

Dive Bar Rating

Back in the early nineties, a freaky Thai spitfire named Sunshine was a big draw at this narrow, photo-collage covered room, located in an area between the "shadier" part of Silver Lake and East Hollywood which some call "Thai Town." Though karaoke has always been an attraction here, this chatty wild child was particularly and uniquely entertaining, especially when you could understand her pearls of wisdom about sex, booze, and life. (If I hadn't been loaded while listening and actually remembered some of them, you'd be reading them here). However, the Cutter's cool factor peaked out around 2000, and though I live about five minutes away, I hadn't been back in several years.

Returning to survey my old hang for this book, I was happy to see that not much had changed over the past decade. The scratchy powdered soap still sprinkled from above the dingy bathroom sink, the old pool table, worn but functional, was still here, and the crowd was singing the same ol' songs (Frampton's "Show Me The Way," Queen's "Bohemian Rhapsody," etc.) Sadly, Sunshine is gone, but the equally bodacious, boozed-out "Mama" Nita still owns the place, demanding that all who enter obey the "mandatory two drink minimum" on karaoke nights (which happens to be almost every night). Non (or slow) imbibers should be prepared to be badgered, belittled, and even kicked out if they don't have a drink in hand (the prices of which often vary within the same night). Ever the dictator, Nita gave me an abrupt arm-squeeze and harsh reprimand for shooting the wild karaoke antics goin' on in the center of the bar, but ceased when I told her the photos were for a book. Soon, she was posing for me with one of her regulars, a handsome lass in leopard print and mounds of beads named Linda (who by the way, does a mean version of "Sympathy for the Devil.") Nita was coy when I probed about the bar's history, but after a few shots and a bootie rubbing grind with a nerdy guy rapping "Baby Got Back," she told me, "I own the bar for over twenty years, and buy it because I an alcoholic!" Don't think I (or you) really need to know more.

Tee Gee

3210 Glendale Blvd.
Phone: (323) 669-9631

In 1946, Joe Grzybowski, a retired World War II vet, and his pal Neal Tracy opened Tee Gee, the name of which refers to the beginning consonants of each man's last name. Unfortunately, the "G" on the bar's huge neon sign looks like a "Y," which means those who've only driven by probably assume the place is some kind of Asian restaurant (At least that's what I always thought).

Now owned by the colorful Miss Betty Barlotta, Grzybowski's girlfriend at the time of his death in 1984, Tee Gee has many tales to tell, and if she's in the right mood 'ol Bette will regale ya with one or several. If not, there's no shortage of newspaper clippings on the walls to fill you in. Among the more colorful stories from the bar's past include a robbery in the '50's that left one customer dead, two fires (after the second one, Betty rebuilt against her insurance company's advice) and the recently celebrated sixtieth anniversary, at which time Betty added some off kilter décor additions, including pencil drawings of 1940's dames. Despite the drawings, the look of Tee Gee is pretty plain: forest green booths lining one wall, and a smattering of Betty Boop memorabilia (gifts from Barlotta's regulars), all under a crusty lime green ceiling complete with gold glitter specks. Ceramic lamps, brown paneling and some mirrors complete the simple, crazy aunt's living room feel. Though I admittedly never set foot in this place until researching this book, my visits always seemed to offer the same cross section of sports buffs gaping blankly at the tube, college types having another birthday party (bad supermarket cake and all) as they filled the jukebox with Guns n' Roses, and lonely, long in the tooth types who had nowhere else to go. Atwater Village may be an up and coming neighborhood, but Tee Gee isn't where the Prius-driving and hip bike-riding brigades go. You get the feeling it will never get too trendy, either. The Betties just won't let it. Both of them.

Tiki Ti

4427 W Sunset Blvd.
Phone: (323) 669-9381

Dive Bar Rating

While this itsy bitsy Hawaiian hut gets dive points off for its super-pricy drink menu ($10-$18) and Vegas gauche LCD screens touting the fruity-tooty concoctions, it's hard to rag on this knick knack-packed shack, especially when the owner, Mike Buhen, tells you that he took the bar over from his dad, Ray, a "legendary mixologist" who helped pioneer the tropical drink craze while working at the famed restaurant Don the Beachcomber, and that his sons, Mark (a barback) and Mike Jr. (checking IDs at the door) both work here. Suddenly, you've got a warm, familial feel... or maybe it's just the voodoo potion disguised as a frou-frou drink you're sipping.

As I said, the drinks may be expensive here (bring the green, it's cash only), but these Hawaiian punches do pack a big one. You wont find wine or beer, but there are ninety different drinks to choose from, most with rum, some with gin, some with tequila, some with vodka and some with all of the above. Of course the rum ones have the coolest names: Cobra's Fang, Skull and Bones, Uga Booga (its name is chanted as its being made), Bonnie and Clyde, Pain Killer and on and on. Mike cut to the chase on the bar's surprisingly info-packed, hi-tech website revealing, "Ray's Mistake" as the most popular drink and "The Stealth" as strongest choice.

Now, video menus and fancy websites may not be exactly divey, but mixing lethal libations in a tiny dilapidated structure that's only slightly more stable than an old tee-pee for almost fifty years kinda trumps everything else. The Ti is the ultimate tropical dive despite whatever attempts it's made at promoting itself with technology. Amidst the hula-infused hullabaloo, dangling lit up blowfish, exotic masks, hundreds of tacky island souvenirs, and butt-filled red ashtrays (a loophole in the law regarding owner-operated and staffed establishments allows Mike and Co. to ignore the cigarette ban) there's real history in this little room. Every Wednesday, Mike pays tribute to Ray, ringing a bell five times, and having everyone in the bar stop what they're doing to toast his pops. And, like Miceli's in Hollywood, which lets you leave your mark on the place via a Chianti bottle and a black Sharpie to be hung in the place for eternity, Buhen lets regulars he deems deserving leave their names and or comments on cards that he posts on the upper wall, aka the "persons of rare character board." Reading these cards is more fun than ogling all the chotchkees in the space combined.

Bigfoot Lodge

LOS FELIZ

Bigfoot Lodge

3172 Los Feliz Blvd.
Phone: (323) 662-9227

Dive Bar Rating

Some will surely groan about the inclusion of this rustic cocktail cabin in this book. Though the Bigfoot Lodge won a highly-touted "Best Dive Bar" contest via the web and local TV station, NBCLA. com, in 2009, many were up in arms about it being labeled a dive. To my thinking, however, Bigfoot, which also celebrated its tenth anniversary in 2009, earns merit as a dive bar for several reasons: cheap PBR, cheesy fun décor, mighty liquor mixes (I almost always have to buy peanuts here to sober up before leaving) and a crowd that is never—despite lots of trendy togs and tattoos—too cool for school.

Bikers from a nearby Harley Davidson store, rockers from all over, inked Fonzie and Pinky Tuscadero lookalikes and casual Joes from the surrounding neighborhoods like Atwater and Silver Lake converge at this warm and woodsy room, known for DJ nights celebrating rock music both classic and obscure (Most spin vinyl too). While Bigfoot lacks the stench and soiled quality of traditional dives, because of the crowd (and those crazy strong drinks) it never ceases to have a rowdy atmosphere, especially around midnight. Toasted marshallow drinks, barmaids in punky girl scout uniforms and Summer Camp-y touches throughout like a giant Smoky the Bear, even bigger than the Sasquatch sign and faux fireplace, contribute to the scene. My favorite night is Rock n' Roll Karaoke Monday, a loud and proud celebration of riff-heavy sounds and bad vox. I had my thirty-third birthday party during the sing-off one evening, and brought the house down with an innovative and awesome rendition of "I Love Rock n' Roll." At least, I think it was awesome—I don't remember much else from the night (as it should be) but pals recall that I took the "Lodge" part of the bar's name a little too literally, going comatose and "camping" out in a back corner. Any bar that lets ya pass out discreetly 'til your posse is ready to leave—as opposed to promptly kicking you out, as they do at nicer clubs—earns eternal brownie dive points with me.

The Dresden

1760 N. Vermont Ave.
Phone: (323) 665-4294

Dive Bar Rating

Yes, this is the bar from *Swingers*. And yes, geriatric lounge duo Marty and Elayne are still alive and kicking (as of this writing), playing every Tuesday thru Saturday, beginning at 9 p.m. sharp. And yes again, the place still gets packed, and it's easy to see why, as the Dresden's Rat Packy atmosphere is undeniable, both in the restaurant (snow white booths, dark wood posts, spiraling chandeliers) and in the main bar (frosted art deco glass, tacky brick, wood, and cork paneling). The eatery part is actually quite sumptuous, though those who chomp here either have hair that matches the booths or do it for the sheer irony factor: no matter how pseudo swanky it may be, or edible the food is (surf and turf is the specialty), it's just a little too retro to take seriously—think *Playboy After Dark*.

Back to Marty and Elayne, the most familiar faces at Dresden. They've been lounging it up here for nearly two decades now, and as Trent, Vince Vaughn's character in *Swingers*, would say, "they are still so money." Often dressed in matching sequins, this raven-tressed duo is definitely the big draw, taking up the middle of the entire bar room with their giant piano and drum set up. The pair have an unmatched enthusiasm for the ol' old jazz standards, not to mention random disco ("I Will Survive" and "Stayin' Alive.") Elayne rocks the keys like a hurricane and Marty aint too shabby on the drums either. More kitschy than anything else, the Dresden nevertheless meets my criteria for inclusion as a dive thanks to its old school style, cheap, strong drinks (try their signature Blood and Sand), and 'tude-filled 'tenders and staff; the waitresses have no qualms about making you move your ass up if you don't adhere to the two drink minimum ($15 on a card).

The Drawing Room

1800 Hillhurst Ave.
Phone: (323) 665-0135

Dive Bar Rating

The Drawing Room enjoys the distinction—at least according to owner Monte Quan—of offering the earliest liquid "breakfast" in the Silver Lake/ Los Feliz area. For over 35 years, 7 days a week, 365 days a year ("even during holidays and the LA riots"), this family-owned bar has opened at 6 a.m., a practice Quan's dad Luke started when he opened the place. Even at that early hour, the bar does descent business, thanks in part to its Los Feliz location being a frequent TV and movie background locale. Film crews, graveyard shifters and insomniac alcoholics count on this modest li'l room to serve up crack of dawn drinks to help them start off the day—or wind down the night. Quan told me there's also a small celeb set that often creeps in to get away from the glare and blare of the A-list spots. Lindsay Lohan is particularly fond of the room, and Quan recalled one incident where the stalkerazzi followed her here and turned the mini-mall, which includes a laundermat also owned by Quan, into complete mayhem. Being the good dive proprietor he is, Quan had 'em all towed.

It's not hard to see why stars seeking solace choose the Drawing Room. With its Asian massage parlor look (a giant dragon replaced a map of the U.S. several years ago on the main wall and random red lanterns are strewn about), its dim hues, and friendly pourers, the place is just chill. And so is the crowd. Young and old, stylish and not so much, the people who come here seem like they couldn't give a crap about who else is here; they're occupied with their own little cliques either at the electronic dartboard, watching the TV above the bar, or in the broken-in booths. Even with the occasional Lohan sighting, it's not cliquey in the lunch room *Mean Girls* sense, though ironically, I do always seem to run into someone I went to high school with here (My alma mater, John Marshall High School, a handsome brick building seen in many commercials and films, is nearby). The Drawing Room is a place you go with friends to get the most splash for your cash (only), with prices starting $3.50. (Tip: try Mario's Grape Ape Shot, delish, cheap, purple and double poured for five dollars). This room's not about hooking up, or showing off your trendy outfit like at most bars in the area, and that is precisely why it keeps drawing no nonsense drinkers in.

The Roost

Dive Bar Rating

If you're averse to the pick-up "artistry" that's enveloped a lot of the bar scene in LA, the Roost is your kind of place... no cock blocking cohorts necessary. It's one of the laxest bars in the city, a raggedy, barn red-hued spot made for nesting and nursing your poison. It's always hospitable, no matter what kind of shoes you're wearing (you'll see flip-flops here all the time), how much dough ya got (drinks are cheap, just bring cash) or who you know (you can come here solo and not feel like a dweeb if you're a dude, or like you're on display if you're a dame).

Los Feliz Blvd. is pretty mild-mannered compared with other happening nightlife hives, but the drinking holes on the street are in close enough proximity to make the area just east of Griffith Park a bonafide bar crawl. The Bigfoot Lodge, The Griffin (divey before a medieval makeover) and the Tam O'Shanter Inn (old fashioned but too frilly for dive consideration) all offer unique drinking environments, but The Roost is the least self-involved. The tube is always on during weeknights, and the bartenders (particularly the unfussy biker-mama here most of the time) usually pay it more attention than you will. If you come here for conversation with a date or group, park it in one of the roomy booths or in the spacious area to the left of the bar (the seating set-up—and large kitchen visible upon entry—suggest the nice sized restaurant this spot was back in the day).

Customers crow for the private parking lot; free popcorn (and not stale bowls that have been sitting on the bar since god knows how long, but from an actual old fashioned machine that you serve yourself from in tiny brown paper bags); a curious plastic partition that divides the room in half, giving privacy to the drinking in the booth area; the non-functioning phone booth cubby hole near the entrance (great for making out); the back wall, lined with dozens and dozens of empty booze bottles; and a human fixture in the form of an elderly Asian gent, who sits at the corner next to the kitchen night after night chewing the fat, literally and figuratively...they're pretty mellow about letting people bring food inside. If you do bring eats here, go Kentucky fried.

LOS FELIZ

LOS ANGELES'S BEST DIVE BARS

Ye Rustic Inn

1831 Hillhurst Ave.
Phone: (323) 662-5757

It's hard to say what the Rustic is better known for: the post-hang-over, hair-of-the-dog scrumptiousness of its Bloody Mary breakfast, or the bloodshot-eyed presence of its most famous regular, *24* star Kiefer Sutherland. While Sutherland's Rustic antics are the stuff of gossip legend, I've seen him here a few times just chillin' at the bar with a pal. It's easy to see why a famous actor would come here; it's one of those dank unassuming rooms that seems oblivious to time of day, or year for that matter. The jukebox is chock with prog and classic rock kings (Led Zeppelin, Journey, Foreigner), the waitresses have a Flo "kiss my grits" quality, and the tube is always transmitting some competitive sport that gets the rough and tumbler types rubber necking, and during big games, 'ahootin' and 'ahollerin.' The décor seems pretty much unchanged since the place opened in 1971, consisting mainly of liquor-sponsor neon and branded knick-knacks, though there's some nifty deer antler chandeliers that keep it from being completely generic.

Tucked inside a mini-mall next to an insurance agency and Chinese food joint, the Rustic, like the Drawing Room across the street (where Kiefer has also been known to pop by) has two distinct crowds depending on when you go. On weekends, you'll find young, hip types sporting tight threads and bright, bushy tailed demeanors. The atmosphere is fun and upbeat, but it can get irritatingly packed. Weeknights, you'll get a less self-conscious mix, older gents and dames, entertainment industry types, sports buffs, and local grubbers. Indeed, the Rustic's mouth-watering bar food menu is cited by many as the best greasy grub in town. Their chili fries, fish and chips, and legendary hot wings may have more admirers than their booze. The later really live up to the hype too; spicy meaty, tender li'l suckers drenched in slurpy, messy red sauce (medium, hot and deadly). I literally used about twenty napkins while noshing on 'em. Kiefer apparently likes 'em too, as his most infamous, much-blogged about visit concerned a 9 a.m. tab of J&B on the rocks and the Inn's beloved wings. Allegedly he left the place without paying his tab, the floor "littered with chicken bones." Drunken karate kicks were also involved. Whether this tale is true doesn't much matter; the Rustic is the kind of place that, celebrity or not, such behavior just ain't that unusual.

Little Bar

KOREATOWN
and
MIRACLE MILE

Frank N Hanks

518 S. Western Ave.
Phone: (213) 383-2087

Aside from the stylized sign out front, Frank N Hanks isn't much to look at: The usual plastic-wood walls, medium-sized bar with a row of stools, electronic dartboard and rear area pool table. However, what makes Frank N Hanks the kind of dive you go back to again and again is the person behind the bar, a pint-sized forty-something Vietnamese lady named Snow. The proprietor and head pour mistress at Frank N Hanks, Snow has lots of friends and fans (including real life Swinger Vince Vaughn) as well as a crew of regulars who make sure nothing bad goes down. Snow bought the place fifteen years ago from the original owners, named, yup, Frank and Hank, and she didn't change much, which has helped her to retain the regulars from way back…way, way back. Though rumors of the Rat Pack hanging here are false, the place was a second home to local comic Timmie Rogers, a ground-breaking black comedian who happened to be buds with none other than Sammy Davis Jr. (a picture of the pair still hangs on the wall). Rogers frequented FnH up until he died in 2006.

I got Rogers' story, and another anecdote about the sole piece of art in the place (a beguiling nude near the entrance; both the artist and the baring babe were regulars) from a friendly young fella named Quinn, whose been going to the bar since he was of drinking age. Like Snow's super-friendly niece Layla (who sometimes helps out on busy nights) Quinn seems right at home in this shabby yet never unsafe room. Because of its Koreatown location, the people-mix is a real ethnic and cross-generational mottle: older African-American gents sitting alone, lost in their own thoughts and oblivious to the gab around them, Asian locals in for a zippy sip after—or during—work, Latina prowler types in low-cut tops scoping the room, and most noticeably, a funky rocker crowd. Famed music venue The Wiltern Theatre is up the street, so you're more likely to see the latter at night after a performance lets out. (It's actually quite amusing to meander about the room and listen to the various post-concert "reviews.") Getting to know Snow is impossible on big gig Wiltern nights, as I found out upon a recent visit after a PJ Harvey show. She's like an energizer bunny behind that bar, eyeing everyone in the place to make sure nobody has to wait a millisecond for their libation, which by the way run in the $4-$6 range and have absurdly generous booze-to-juice/mix ratios. It might be a dive, but Frank N Hanks is the kind of dive your mom might run—if your mom was a middle-aged Vietnamese woman: clean, welcoming and bullshit free.

HMS Bounty

3357 Wilshire Blvd.
Phone: (213) 385-7275

You can literally smell the Bengay in this old-timey, nautical vessel, especially during the day, when seasoned fillies and fellas blow their social security checks on their daily liquid lunch. Okay, this characterization may not be exactly fair—HMS has an expansive menu and most who come here during the daylight hours are eating (steak, salads, fish and chips and oldy heart-attack plates like Monte Cristos)—but still, there's no denying HMS's granny-friendly environs, which are enhanced by the kitschy seafaring interior (dusty old pictures of ships and stuff) and its anchored spot at the bottom of the divine Deco live-in hotel, The Gaylord (which you get to tour—and maybe even get lost in—if you attempt to go to the restroom).

The bar, which stands across the street from the site of the former Ambassador Hotel and up from where the historic Brown Derby once packed in patrons, dates back to 1920s, calling itself Dale's Secret Harbor until the 1960s. It has gone through the hot-and-not dive cycle several times since, but its heyday was definitely right after owner Gordon Fields (who passed away in 1998) took it over in 1962 and christened it the Bounty. Everyone from Duke Ellington to Jack Webb (the *Dragnet* star, who still has a plaque near his old table) were regulars. Despite new owners, it looks as if nothing has changed inside since those jazzy snazzy ol' days. A dusty vintage, record playing jukebox is still in a corner, though sadly it no longer plays, so the sounds are provided by the requisite digital player.

The current crowd is a mixture of lanky-hip, bespectacled boys in retro sweaters (the kind that collect records and drink Old Fashioneds and Gimlets), random couples looking to get frisky in its back room's red leather booths, and as we previously stated, old people. Really cool, sometimes way too chatty old people—be prepared to maneuver your way out of a long conversation if you do strike one up with one of the old-timers. However, don't expect the same of the staff. The bar babes I've encountered have been near-mute, but then, they're probably settled in their roles as captive audience to the regulars nightly tales of bygone eras. Speaking of which, HMS has been featured in the hot retro TV hit, *Mad Men*, providing an authentic milieu for the show's early sixties slice of Americana, not surprisingly, best known for its characters drink-centric lifestyles.

Little Bar

757 S. La Brea Ave.
Phone: (323) 937-9210

This La Brea pit isn't particularly puny compared with other neighborhood bars, but the name is apropos, as the place *feels* small and intimate, with a chill-laxed atmosphere that is reflected in the no frills look of the bar: red brick popping thru (intentionally?) peeling paint on the walls, sportsy touches (the owner is obviously from Boston), old school video games (on a sitdown newbie machine), and a very popular dart board in back. Beer, wine and Soju (the bar's signature drinks, "Skinny Bitch" and the Soju Car Bomb, are made with the latter) make up the menu, along with a nice and fairly priced tap selection, many of which go great with eats from nearby restaurants like the beefy boite Unami Burger, which you can bring in. A lot of bars allow outside grub, but only a handful of them actually create an environment in which you want to do so, as food aromas can be distracting, and the patrons at many dives will let you know it too. With its spacious wooden benches, lively air, and un-selfconscious regulars, a little charbroil smell won't bother anyone here, and a big burger with a side of Little Bar makes for a satisfying combo.

The Little Bar is a good place to hit alone—especially if you're on your way to the nearby 10 Freeway around rush hour and want to sit out the traffic for an hour or so. It's real easy to get enveloped by the flow of conversation, which gets more and more interesting as the evening goes on. A pack of yuppie chaps argue the age old mystery—what women want—near the front of the bar ("size matters!" the most impudent pecker announces just loud enough for everyone in the room to hear), while a guy and gal on a date of some sort awkwardly dance around topics like the online file-sharing controversy and the merits of iPhones (wonder if they met on Match.com?) near the back of the room. This mix of twenty and thirty-something Facebook-user types is typical these days, as the lonely miscreants and horny misfits that used to frequent the spot when it was called Girl Talk (a taxi dancer dive which had one of my all-time favorite signs, covered with red lip marks) have pretty much been gone since the place went Little in 2005.

One Eye Jacks

3977 Beverly Blvd.
Phone: (323) 669-9302

Dive Bar Rating

To quote the Korean lady who owns the place, "You American... you special!" Yup, Caucasians are the minority inside this kill-you-with-boredom beer and wine-only box, but despite the proprietress and her attempts at English for my benefit—not to mention the bar's Koreatown adjacent locale—One Eye (no "D") is not a Korean club-house, but an Espanol casa. Despite its jazzy moniker (owner tells me the place is thirty years old and had the name before her family took it over about a dozen years ago...at least that's what I think she said), this boite is beyond bland, at least for non-Spanish speakers. It's brightly lit with puke-ish colored walls, red tables and chairs, a pool table that the owner uses as a makeshift desk, KMEX on the fuzzy TV, ranchero and Spanish ballads on the jukebox, and random regulars that may or may not be legal (and I mean that in more ways than one...no one checks IDs, at least not early on weeknights). The beer selection is decent if not cheaper than usual: $4 for a Corona, served with a paper plate full of sliced lime and a pile of salt packets, ala Tops Club. The wine is another story: there's just one brand and it's of the five dollar giant jug variety. Amidst Beverly Blvd.'s bounty of carnicerias and 99 Cents "and above" bargain stores, the bar's bright yellow sign definitely pops, and driving by, I often wondered what kind of intoxicated intrigue might be taking place inside. Now I know (and so do you): *nada*.

Powerhouse

HOLLYWOOD

The Bar

5851 Sunset Blvd.
Phone: (323) 468-9154

If you visited Hollywood a decade or two ago, and then came back today, you wouldn't recognize it. The boulevard of broken dreams lost its gloss and glamour around the mid-80s, and it has taken millions of dollars and almost two decades to get it back to what it once was, or at least a developer's idea of what it once was; the area is more like Times Square in New York these days than the seedy starlet-specked Tinseltown of yore. Jumbotrons, mall shops, fast food joints and swanky nightclubs might help the Cali economy by bringing in the tourists, but they've also brought some serious traffic problems to the area, as well as taking away some of its character. While some miss the days when Hollywood Blvd. and Sunset Blvd. saw more hookers, pimps and homeless than hotties in halter tops and dads in Bermuda shorts, for better or worse, Hollywood today is an amalgamation of old and new, with lots of redo's.

It's been over five years since the ravaged Hollywood dive known as The Ski Room (which definitely saw its share of white stuff-induced wipe-outs) was recreated as The Bar. Under its old moniker, the place used to be one of the most tragic spots in town: smarmy barflies and Hollywood junkie-types dozing on rickety stools or shooting away their days on the even ricketier pool table. When it became The Bar, the new owners definitely spruced things up, but thankfully didn't go too far. The place is still a no frills drinking hole; small, dark and simple, with leather booths, nice lighting fixtures and an impressive bottle selection (the drinks are good, but not exactly cheap). Despite the lack of puke and duke-outs, there's something about the current incarnation that still retains the old Ski Room unpredictability. Of course, the Sunset Blvd. location, next to a busy Mobil gas station and a sleazy (ho)tel, is a big part of it. I don't think I've ever been spared a vociferous "compliment," or two when walking through the bright-lit pump place next to the bar, or when crossing Sunset. It's like all the loud-mouthed douchebags in town converge at that corner. Fortunately, not many of these catcalling cretins actually get into The Bar, as the bouncer earns his pay keeping the local riff-raff out.

A vortex for fashionably loud types since pretty much the day it re-opened, boring name and all, The Bar's lack of a sign (there is an awning with an address) was seen by many as pretentious, but I've always found it fitting. A big gaudy sign just doesn't make sense here, aesthetic-wise or attitude-wise. Its down-low approach is in fact why it remains a popular place, that and its weekly DJ nights. The best one is also the longest running: Bent Mondays, a music-mash featuring some of the most notable spinners in the city, DJ Adam 12, Sean Patrick, Zach Rosencrantz and Chris Holmes. That night, and on weekends, The Bar gets uncomfortably crammed, and the poor excuse for a smoking patio (it's a slice of pavement) and bad bathroom placement can cause major gridlock. Those with personal space issues should check out the place on weeknights, which are roomier, more relaxed, but just as rockin' soundtrack-wise.

The Burgundy Room

1621 1/2 N. Cahuenga Blvd.
Phone: 323-465-7530

When it comes to the new Hollywood hop, no street rivals the congested chaos of Cahuenga Blvd. The street was officially dubbed a "corridor" a few years ago, but seasoned clubbers and anyone who's ever tried to get from Hollywood Blvd. to Sunset Blvd. via the two-block stretch on weekends have another name for it: clusterfuck. Currently, the hotspot roll on Cahuenga includes The Beauty Bar, The Room, Delux, Ecco, Kitchen 24, Velvet Margarita, Citizen Smith, and Hotel Café (and there're even more clubs on the north side of Hollywood Blvd). The first two come just short of being dive bars (Beauty, which has sister spots in New York, Austin and Las Vegas, is too eye shadow-sparkly/retro-kitschy to be a real dive, though in comparison to the other biz's on the street, it almost makes the cut, while The Room, a once hidden alley entry cave and one of the few places that blatantly ignored the smoking ban when it came into effect, *was* the quintessential dive until a remodel a few years ago). The rest are glossy new establishments that attract a mix of tourists and weekend warriors. But there are two exceptions on this brisk little boulevard: The Spotlight and the rock n' roll hole known as The Burgundy Room.

The Burgundy Room had many names since first opening its doors in 1919; it was most famously known in the '40s as Ma and Pa Henderson's (the prop of bandleader Skitch Henderson and his wife, Miss America Faye Emerson). In the '60s and '70s, the space was called Tommy's, and in the '80s, Dave's Cave. The place was bought and rechristened The Burgundy Room in 1989, ushering in a new era of low-key bars in the area that included the now-closed Lava Lounge, 3 Clubs, and The Room. When The Burgundy Room was taken over by a former regular a couple of years ago, he, thankfully, didn't change a thing. The place is still so dark your pupils shrink upon entering, and the black-garbed crowd melds into the scenery like creatures in a spooky cave. Ear-busting music and bawdy behavior are the name of the game when DJs spin the likes of The Stones, Bowie, and KISS. A few of my pals spin here, and I have to confess to some screeching devil horn hand-signing of my own when a particularly big anthem blasts out of the sound system. The raw punky feel of this place heightens even a subtle buzz, and the music often takes it to a keg party level. The fact that the space is super-narrow makes things, especially, uh, cozy too.

On weekends, it gets downright cramped, which is why the front entrance outside is as popular as the bar itself—that and the fact that the Burg seems to attract a heavy smoking crowd. If you can stand the nicotine clouds, this busy entry way is actually an amusing place to hang. The bar's much beloved doorman Torrance Jackson (a local blues musician and all around cool dude) is always there to chat, give advice and often, cause a little ruckus. His philosophy on doormanning sort of epitomizes the Burgundy's rough charm. He once told us his "screening process" for potential troublemakers was to rag at 'em, because if they couldn't take some slags at the door, they probably wouldn't be able to handle as many swigs inside. Sweet talk or shit talk, either way, hanging with T.J. and the bar's freaks and flies outside makes for a sharp contrast with the glitz blitz that now surrounds the place.

Crane's Hollywood Tavern

1611 N El Centro Blvd.
Phone: (323) 467-6600

Dive Bar Rating

Crane's is located directly across the street from the place where I workout (when I workout), the Bally's Total Fitness off of Hollywood Blvd, dubbed affectionately by a few of my friends as "the rock n' roll gym," both for its black hair-dyed members and its vicinity to rollicking Hollywood Blvd. Crane's can be very R&R too, especially during "rock 'n roll bingo" when rock stars (if somewhat faded ones) call the balls and give out prizes like concert tickets and t-shirts. That shindig, as well as local band gigs, take place at night, but the smallish unassuming room and homey backyard-like patio really pumps on Sunday afternoons during the summer, when the bar's most popular promotion, the hip-hop hullabaloo known as The Do-Over takes over. Though I've seen the lines to get into that one while exiting my gym after a grueling workout, I've never popped in for a post (or pre) exercise alcoholic hydration... if I did, now that would be rock n' roll! Still, the Do-Over has capped off a few wild weekends for me over the years, and the exceptional gathering—which features biggie mystery guest DJs every week— surely owes part of its organic feel to the slightly rundown backdrop. The vivacious vibe just wouldn't be the same in some swanky spot (and the promoters know it; apparently there's been attempts at wooing them away from this old Hollywood hut for years). Sunday's specialty is Sangria, and Crane's on any night retains telltale purple stains and splashes here and there, a reminder of just how spirited the soiree gets... and how lazy they are about scrubbing the place. We don't even wanna know what the place looks like on Monday mornings, but we'll bet whoever attempts to clean it has no need for a cardio workout next door.

Relax Pub

5511 Hollywood Blvd.
Phone: (323) 460-6705

This beer and wine spot not only stands at one of the sketchiest intersections in town (Hollywood Blvd. and Western Ave.), it's also right next to a gaudy "Thai" hot dog stand (a giant wiener and bun sits atop its roof) and a porn shop, so it's easy to miss if you're driving by. But if you're a fan of Pad Thai (the place is owned by the takeout spot next door) and heavy metal, and happen to have a strange desire to enjoy both together, then Relax is for you.

You can bring your peanut sauced entree from next door into the bar, and though they don't have hard liquor, the booking here, manned by Eddie Solis (of Southern Lord Recordings) since 2006, is spicier than anything on the door hanger paper menu. Solis has helped make this dungeon-like drink spot a heavy music haven, consistently booking speed metal, punk and other noisy genres. Some nights the music really sucks, but other nights, you almost wonder why the talents you're watching are playing such a sad little dump. The room itself feels almost like an underground loft, anywhere but in the heart of east Hollywood. The stage isn't really even a stage; more like a cubbyhole. The walls are cracked and dreary (though sometimes covered by decent art), and the bartender gals are either really shy or just don't speak English. However, all of these disparities are part of Relax's unconventional buoyancy. There's a nice sized smoking patio out back, which is big enough for even non-smokers to take a breather, and conversations (often about music) are easily struck. Though the crowd may look scary—lots of long hair, black garb and skull-covered accessories—they're a surprisingly jovial bunch. You sort of feel a kinship with fellow Relax-ers when you're there because 1) You're all *there* and not at some fancy hot spot up the street; 2) Believe it or not, head bangers are generally nice people (though there is a horny drunk hesher factor that must be watched out for if you're a female); 3) The regulars may worship Satan (or pretend to for the stage), but the real evils often lie just outside the door.

Frolic Room

6245 Hollywood Blvd.
Phone: (323) 462-5890

Dive Bar Rating

An LA liquor lover's landmark and maybe Hollywood's most famous bar, Bob's Frolic Room served as the private party room to the luminaries who performed at the adjacent Pantages Theatre back in the '30s. More famously, it was a former haunt of tragic starlet Elisabeth Short (*The Black Dahlia*) in the '40s, and Charles Bukowski in the '70s (and is said to have housed the private offices of Howard Hughes in the '50s). Despite the Frolic's colorful history, not to mention attempts to maintain a somewhat formal air (the bartenders and door guy are always spiffily attired in all-black or black and white), and the classic art of Al Hirschfield (known for his caricatures in *The New Yorker*) on the main wall, the glitz of this place faded years ago. Today, it is an old-school dive that on any given night attracts boozy boulevard drifters, punky locals disgusted by new Hollywood's velvet rope mentality, and a hefty dose of out-of-towners drawn both by its vicinity to Hollywood's biggest theatre (productions of which include everything from *The Lion King* to *Wicked* to *Dirty Dancing*) and its eye-catching neon sign.

It's a sliver of a room, with a row of stools running down the center...and that's about it. A jamming jukebox (Bob Marley, The Beatles, etc.) creates some atmosphere, but really, the Frolic is about the people plopped upon its stools and those serving them. I've never had trouble striking up a conversation (or even having to be the first one to do so), but that may be due to the fact that—at least at night—the guy to girl ratio is easily 5 to 1. If you're a lonely lady here by yourself , you'll very likely meet a fella; maybe not Prince Charming, but beggars can't be choosers can they? The room's nostalgic ambience, used to great affect in films such *LA Confidential* and *The Black Dahlia*, sometimes gets lost when it's really packed, so it best not to go after the theatre lets out. I do however, recommend it before catching a concert at the Music Box Theatre up the street, or hitting any club on the boulevard for that matter. The cocktails are twice as potent and almost half the price of most in the area, so it's a great pre-club pitstop.

Back in the early nineties, the Frolic, like many dives, enjoyed a rocker renaissance, with the long-haired, Jack Daniels swigging scene packing the place so consistently the owners opened a second spot up the street on Wilcox Ave. True story: On my very first night out in my very first car (which I saved up for years to buy), I went to the Frolic II with some girlfriends. When I came out of the bar, I saw my beat-up but beloved Camaro being driven away by a thief, who almost hit me as he sped off. Back then getting insurance wasn't Cali law, so I had none. And I never saw the car again. You'd think I'd have given up barhopping all together after that, but of course I didn't. I never did go back to Frolic II (it closed a few years later), but the original will always be a fave. See this book's cover for an eyeful of its superlative neon sign.

Gold Diggers

5632 Santa Monica Blvd.
No Phone

If the 2 Live Crew anthem "Me So Horny" pops into your head at this fetid little freak house, it's not necessarily because you are. In fact, Gold Diggers is more a kinky dinky that a true turn-on, as the Asian ladies on display are the types to say "me love you long time" without much enthusiasm. Whenever I have been here, the featured femmes on stage could not have seemed less interested in their dancing duties; surprisingly, the feeling from the regulars is mutual, as most seem to be ignoring the stage going-ons, which makes the experience of drinking here all the more bizarre.

Gold Diggers is only one of two "strip clubs" included in this book (Jumbo's Clown Room being the other) and that's because both are destination dives as much as they are bikini bars, and being in Hollywood, both have as many hot messes off stage as on (Actually, Jumbo's features real foxes these days, so it's very much Nobu to Digger's Panda Express). Poochy, bitty bods, bushy pits/brows and questionable genders aside, G.D.'s dead-eyed, mostly non-English speaking jigglers are wacky fun, especially when they bust out one of the place's signature tools of seduction: laser pointers! That's right, the Thai temptress's here not only highlight their privates with illuminating pens like they're doing some kind of naughty office presentation, they actually call-out dudes at the bar by shooting 'em right between the eyes—and balls—with the little green lights. Take away the pens and poonanny and here's what you've still got to soak in at G.D.: decently priced and indecently poured drinks, black paint with gold specks everywhere, beat-up brass bars around the tiny stage, chipped floors, mostly Latino gents hanging about (if you're not Asian or Mexican, be prepared for puzzled stares when you walk in) and dance hits sped up so fast on the (broken?) stereo they're almost unrecognizable (I think I actually prefer Black Eyed Peas "Where Is the Love" as sung by the Chipmunks). As adult entertainment, the place is lacking, but as curious dive camp, it's pure gold.

Lotus Lounge

1135 N Vermont Ave.
Phone: (323) 664-8554

Lotus is one of those places that the East Hollywood locals I know always speculate about but never have the gumption to enter, assuming it's an Asian only establishment of some sort. But when I ventured into the grey and red beer and wine grotto, entering through a door covered by a dingy striped curtain under which too-bright-for-a-bar rays of light spilled through, I was surprised to find that most of the crowd was white—peppered with some Thai and Latinos—all of whom were men. Other than the friend I brought with me and the tiny, smiley barmaid behind the counter, it's grubby guyville in here, and judging from the ravenous looks we got, that's usually the case.

The sparse little room has some sponsored neon and a mirrored right side wall, but the most noticeable fixture is behind the bar and it sort of says it all about this one: a big, crookedly hung poster of an awkward-looking Thai babe in bad '80s printed lingerie. Mismatched chairs, the customary Christmas lights, a faded out pool table, new juke and pocked dart board fill in the rear portion of the bar, but its up front with Leilani—that's what I decided to name the girl in the poster—where things get lively in this florescent-lit fiesta. If you like karaoke come here on weekends; there's never a wait for the mic and the selection ain't half bad. If you're a gal, the guy manning the machine will seduce you into singing by putting on girl power numbers ("My Boyfriend's Back," "Girls Just Want to Have Fun") and if you're like me, you will give in eventually, especially since the mic cord is long enough so that you don't even have to leave your stool. It was at Lotus Lounge that I found my new favorite 'oke number in fact: Nancy Sinatra's "Boots." Remember, when crooning for a dive bar full of boys, girls gotta keep things badass.

Jumbo's Clown Room

5153 Hollywood Blvd.
Phone: 323-666-1187

Dive Bar Rating

This legendary (semi) strip club turned bikini bar is a saucy circus of loud, lively music, decent-priced drink, and, of course, dance, and the place's exuberance is unmatched by both nudie spots and traditional dives alike. Despite the occasional perv in the corner, Jumbo's always has a festive, family-feel, which makes sense since it is a family-owned business and has been since first opening in its mini-mall location back in 1970. Owner Karen Taylor took the reigns from her dad Jack—aka Jumbo—in 1990, and she's worked hard to change the place's image and rep over the years. Though it started out as a friendly neighborhood bar, evolved into a disco club and then a country western music bar, the Clown Room is best known for its gentlemen's club era, which began in 1982. Unfortunately, during the late '80's—what Taylor calls the "lean years"—someone else ran the place for her father, and it became known for a caliber of booty shakin' babe that wasn't exactly beguiling. To this day, Courtney Love's time at Jumbo's during her drugged out pre-Kurt Cobain phase gets sighted as an example of the girls here, but, in reality, the trashy, less than fit types are long gone, replaced by lovely, equally rock n' roll–ish lasses (lots of tatted tarts grinding to everything from the Stones to Black Sabbath to David Bowie blasting from the old jukebox) who take their job seriously, showing off true athletic prowess on the pole. Many also have a flair for the dramatic, with theme costumes and theatrics spicing up their moves.

It may not be as captivatingly seedy as it was in the '80s or even before the '04 city ordinance that made the ladies cover up and wear bikinis during their dances, but Jumbos will always have a sexually surreal quality (David Lynch likes to hang here, for godsakes!) In the past few years, Taylor has put in new tables (with colorful clown portraits) and lighting and painted the place, but remnants of Jumbo's past still remain: the filthy bathrooms, the dark corner lapdance area, and a smattering of the dirty old man types salivating at the girls as they work the room after their sets. One of my best gal-pals, a vixen by the name of Michelle, happens to be a longtime bartender here (another reason the place feels so homey... and yes I tackled the pole here once just to see what it was like, but it was after hours). My GF notes a new generation of young, fashionable patrons, particularly on the weekends, for whom the performances on stage almost seem secondary to the bar itself. While this might be tough on the tip-funded livelihoods of Jumbo gyrators, it is a testament to the place, as Jumbo's magic is as much about memories as it about mammaries.

Powerhouse

1714 N Highland Ave.
Phone: (323) 463-9438

Opened by a former Hollywood area barber named Joe Power back in the forties, The Powerhouse is referred to by many as the "last dive bar standing," not so much because it literally is such (only the Frolic and Burgundy are in the vicinity), but because the rundown runt of a room is smack dab inside the voracious vortex of tourist cash trappings that typify Hollywood today. With its corner Jumbotron, pricey shops, movie theatres, nightclubs and the Kodak Theatre (where the Academy Awards are held every year), the Hollywood and Highland Complex pretty much dwarfs everything else around it. A tiny bar like Powerhouse, which stands directly across the street, while inconsequential to those looking for family fun or celeb sightings, is exactly what locals love and those seeking "real" Hollywood should check out. In fact, the place does get its share of famous faces, hiding out from the boulevard's more obvious boites, though the only name they'll drop is The Beatles, who hung here during their historic Hollywood Bowl shows up the street (they stayed at the Holiday Inn across the street) back in '64 and '65.

Manager/partner Jim Kalin says he and the people behind less grungy spots like The Firefly and Match in the Valley took over the place in 2004, banishing the druggie element and "making it safe for girls to come in alone" again. Well, *groups* of girls anyway. When I popped by on a Thursday night with a girlfriend, we definitely felt ogled by many of the older gents in the place, especially in the back smoking area, which also happen to reek with certain pungent aromas. Still, the crude curmudgeon contingent is always colored-up by tatted punk and goth heads, random foreigners and everything in between. There's even a cool dwarf/little person who knows everyone, adding to the rock n' roll circus feel. Mismatched striped booths complete with indentations of planted rumps past, a sparse and odd smattering of art (a velvet painting of a clown, a baby head painting), requisite holiday lights and a snake of cracked and peeling vinyl that runs, almost design like, along the arm rest above the bar where you order complete the big top slop. A big Power plus: their kickass CD jukebox featuring loads of LA based bands big and small, like The Gun Club, X, The Cramps, and The Red Hot Chili Peppers.

Prime Time

5556 Santa Monica Blvd
Phone: (323) 467-2802

A block up from the scummy splendor of Gold Diggers on Santa Monica Blvd. near Western, you'll find this rather simple, sometimes sleepy hole. And unlike Diggers, which has an audacious yellow sign that surely makes drivers-by curious about the shenanigans going on inside, Prime Time's pea-green storefront "cocktail and karaoke music" signage is easy to miss. I cruised by this bar literally thousands of times and never noticed it…even parked in front of it on my way to 'Diggers once.

The blank n' beaten quality makes Prime Time a perfect choice for film locations; most recently it was seen in the Will Smith flick *Hancock*, during which the lead picks up a trashy lass at the bar and takes her back to his place. Prime Time ain't a pick-up joint in real life by any means, though a slightly hipper, happier crowd does come in for weekend karaoke. As a rule, this olive walled, Hollywood souvenir-swathed space (somebody *really* likes Marilyn Monroe) is much more relaxed on weeknights when the karaoke isn't happening. Even the sassy-ass barmaid seems more chill, as are her regulars. She actually got a gift from a customer during my last visit: a wine glass hand-painted with colorful flowers. She proceeded to show it off to every single person in the pub, while the guy who made it for her cringed and cowered in a corner. In bars like this, some people really want to be noticed, while others really, really don't.

A fella by the name of Fabio (who looks nuthin' like the romance novel guy) mans the bar on karaoke Fridays, and Fab sure knows his dives; he does Saturdays at the seedier, if equally hidden Winchester Room. Singers range from great to ghastly, as per the usual course for these types of things. Always keep in mind that karaoke comes with some rules, no matter where you are: 1) Tip the karaoke guy ($1 or more per song); 2) Come when your name is called (if you're too enraptured in conversation on the smoking patio or primping in the bathroom you may lose your spot); and 3) Order something to drink while you're partaking in the "entertainment." Like Smog Cutter and a couple of other bars in this book, the 'tenders—on these evenings especially—ain't too tender to tell you where to go (as in o-u-t) if you're loitering without liquoring.

Three Clubs

1123 Vine St.
Phone: (323) 462-6441

Dive Bar Rating

🍾🍾

Three things must said right off the bat about Three Clubs: 1) Despite what most clueless types (even locals) call it, it's name is NOT the Three OF Clubs; 2) It is dark... maybe too dark; 3) It is loud...definitely too loud. Owner Marc Smith opened this, at one time, "It" spot in 1991, and though it seemed somewhat swanky when I first started coming here back then, over the years, it has definitely dived down. One of the first bars to forgo signage in favor of a more low-key exterior, this mini-mall fave suffered a blow to its bizarroness when they took down the infamous "Bargain Clown Mart" sign from its previous incarnation, a rusty ol' eyesore that had been on the roof for years (It was/is still how most travel guides, Hollywood blogs, etc. tip tourists on how to find the place).

With that ironic reminder of the past gone, Clubs' exterior seems a lot cleaner, making its inclusion here a bit iffy. Naysayers will say the booths are too taut and shiny, and the wood paneling too nice (nothing carved in it). The carpet—from what you can see in the darkness— isn't too scary either, but I'm sure it would be another story under bright lights, or worse, black lights. Despite a seemingly diligent cleaning staff, scents of a room sometimes tell a story. The shaggy denim and leather crowd that frequent on weeknights (more so than the weekend mallrats) can be defiant when it comes to the smoking ban, and I've seen both cocktails and tossed cookies fly onto the floor when things got crowded and or a little crazy, both in the main bar (in which a blaring, mostly rock-filled jukebox adds to the cacophony) and the adjacent room, where everything from rock bands to burlesque dancers perform.

Three more things to note about Three Clubs: 1) You can park—usually for free—in the adjacent mini-mall lot (which includes a massage parlor!); 2) It was in the movie *Swingers*, which was spot-on about L.A. clubber's aversion to car-pooling, which means you'll be lucky to score a space in the lot after 10 p.m.; 3) The security guards are big and bull-ish. And they should be; this corner of Santa Monica Blvd. and Vine St. not only sees a lot of, um, trans-actions (as in transsexual hook-ups for cash), but with so many hot spots nearby, those who couldn't get in anywhere else often end up here, and those juiced-up jokers can get wild on weekends, and not in a good way. Weeknights, though, Three Clubs will always be a winning hand.

Sexy Sipping

Jumbos Clown Room

Sardos

The Embers

Footsies

Whisperz

Gold Diggers

The Spotlight

1601 N. Cahuenga Blvd.
Phone: (323) 467-2425

This "delightfully crummy place" (as printed own its own business card) is surely looked upon by many as Cahuenga Blvd.'s ugly sore thumb, a fungus-y, old, unsightly thing that just won't go away and which you can't really ignore no matter how hard you try. (It stands on the street's liveliest corner, at Selma, after all.) An austere reminder of Hollywood's less-greedy past, The Spotlight holds on today thanks to 80-year-old owner Don Samuels, who refuses to succumb to persistent fat-pocketed promoters and nightlife impresarios fiending for its prime locale. Samuels, a frail, pale, newsboy-capped chap, can be found pretty much every night at his perch next to the bar's front door, planted on a stool and clutching who knows what in a plastic market bag.

The bar is usually not very packed when I pop in (which I try to do whenever I'm on the street), and the people who are here are always friendly, if often a bit bonkers. Décor-wise it's pretty nondescript: beige walls, lots of neon beer promo signs, some mirrors, a pool table in the back room. Though its ragged feel should make Spotlight appeal to the same rebellious, anti-swank revelers who frequent The Burgundy Room up the street, it doesn't, mostly because it's known as a gay dive (Next to the "Established in 1963" printed on its blue awning out front, there's a rainbow flag). Walking into this place, despite a long-standing sketchy rep, I've never felt worried or unwelcomed (which I can't say about some of the nicer gay spots I've been to, many of which seem to equate "vagina" with "vile"). At least these days, Spotlight, which isn't nearly as lowlit as most dives, ain't scary at all. The bartenders are sweet and pour even sweeter (cocktails run about $4-$6), gay men have crooned for me (on karaoke night), bi-boys have hit on me (but not too hard), trannies have given me fashion tips and I've been treated to some of the most fascinating bar chatter ever. I even made a friend here, an old broad who lives at a rent-by-the week hotel in the area. For a couple shots of bourbon, this dame (who asked not to be identified) sits next to me on a stool at the bar and tells me intoxicated tales of her former career as an actress and showgirl in Vegas. With her garish Bette Davis make-up and old Hollywood speak (every sentence ends with "dah-ling"), my new pal is a dive bar character in the truest sense. Meandering through H'Wood daily, she says the upscale changes have been hard for her. Newer bars, she complains, have dismissed or ignored her patronage. But not The Spotlight. "All the fancy places around here can be very, very mean, dahling," she says. "But this place is great and the boys who come here, they're my brothers."

Vine Bar

1235 Vine St.
Phone: (323) 871-4060

Whether dolled up as the avocado-green retro fondue boite that it was when it first opened, dolled down as the black swathed rock pit it became afterwards, or the sexily simple chandeliered room it is today, Vine Bar's convivial grit stays the same. And while this may be mostly about its location (in between Hollywood Blvd.'s club mad bustle and Santa Monica Blvd.'s boy toy hustle) VB itself has seen its share of crazy shenanigans over the years, with its first two incarnations failing, so the gossip goes, due to substance problems, staff/owner conflicts and straight up skirmishes near the entrance, in which gunshots were not an unfamiliar sound.

None of that seems to be an issue currently. The rocker types who've taken it over really have made it a chill neighborhood room, though thankfully they've left some of the punky touches from the previous incarnation intact, namely the junkyard-ish dance room in which one wall is lined with old television sets (some working and showing groovy old movies). A very narrow front column along the bar leads you to a backroom which is lit just so, hence inspiring some major arm and leg flailing, especially when DJs spin, rock or electro depending on the night. There was a point back in 2005 when Vine was *the* spot, particularly on Thursdays. I did a piece about its hip hub status for the *LA Times*, but—shocker—soon after, it got a little too hip. They instituted passwords for entry, but the secret was out, and that coupled with the aforementioned management drama saw the place lose its pizzazz. It shut down for several months and was re-opened by the current proprietors rather quietly. What you should know about it now: the drinks are moderately priced, but potently poured; the 'tenders are usually attractive band dudes and dudettes; and the upstairs loft, which used to be open all the time and saw some very *Boogie Nights*-like behavior during the previous proprietorships, is usually closed off.

White Horse

1532 N Western Ave.
Phone: (323) 462-8088

Dive Bar Rating

While the "rse" from this infamous Western Ave. dive's sign is often burnt out, me and my buds have been calling this place "the white 'ho" since back when the lights still worked. Don't let our nickname fool ya though: while the bar is smack in the middle of one of the grungiest streets in Los Angeles, this ho ain't cheap, at least not anymore. Drinks were a deal here before the remodel that occurred after the Northridge Earthquake in 1994, but today a cocktail is in the $8 range, and they're not always the most robust. However, there's still reason to gallop into this dingy cash only den, which stands just below a trick-busy Super 8 Motel. The feast-like free food spread every night for one: endless popcorn, pretzels, cookies and candies can be found on platters near the main bar, and free hot dogs come out most eves around 8 p.m. Another plus is that the place's recreation-center roomy, with more seating (mismatched, grandma-ish couches and chairs) than any other dive in town. If you're like me and you hate awkward standing room only hot spots, or worse the buffoonery of the bottle service phenom, especially after you're nice and lightheaded from your favorite libation, this is a good 'un for ya. You can almost always sit and gingerly sip here to your liver's (dis)content.

The tacky living room look, pool table in the center of the room, and nicely packed juke make the 'Ho a long-time favorite for birthday parties (like The Smog Cutter, it can easily be invaded). Birthdays and various bashes past have been immortalized on the back walls via snapshots, and there's so many it would literally take hours to ogle 'em all (I always get bored—and blurry-eyed—before I finish). "Mama" aka Vicki Lelea, the brawny Russian lass who owns the joint is an acquired taste, tough but maternal, generous (with food not booze) but not exactly nice or forthcoming. When I asked for some background on the place and the remodel, which I heard she did after divorcing her hubby who owned the bar previously, she told me she didn't want to talk, handed me a plate of Keebler snacks and walked away. Anyone remember that song "White Horse" by Laid Back? "If you wanna be rich, you got to be a bitch." I always leave here humming that one, for some reason.

Barney's Beanery

WEST HOLLYWOOD
and
SUNSET STRIP

Barney's Beanery (bar area)

8447 Santa Monica Blvd.
Phone: (323) 654-2287

Dive Bar Rating

Smack in the middle of boys town but decidedly straight and even slightly uncouth crowd-wise, Barney's might be the biggest, diviest restaurant in all of LA (definitely in WeHo). Founded in 1920 as a pitstop along historic Route 66 (now known as Santa Monica Blvd.) that did in fact serve beans as its specialty, the place was popular with truckers, bikers and travelers in its early days, then later on with thespians such as Clark Gable, Errol Flynn, and Judy Garland, and eventually, with sixties era Sunset Strip fixtures such as Jim Morrison, Jimi Hendrix and Janis Joplin, (who is said to have boozed up here the night she died). Charles Bukowski was also a regular, and there was a surprisingly artsy contingent—considering the joint's redneckish feel—including Ed Ruscha and Ed Kienholz, whose well-known sculpture piece "The Beanery" remains one of his most discussed both for its olfactory facets (it smelled like beer) and the patrons within the tableu (women in ratty, stained coats, men practically passing out).

These days, Barney's may not be the first place that comes to mind when one thinks of a dive (it became a chain several years ago, and its sister restaurants and bars are very Hooters-like), but this location, particularly the bar area, still fits the bill. I've seen it all here. From rukus' over its controversial "Fagots, Stay Out" (yes, they spelled it wrong) sign, which was ultimately taken down for good by gay rights activists in the '80s, to groupie grind-a-thons during the "metal years." If the place itself had an ignorant vibe back then, today it's more the crowd that qualifies: loud, barf-happy bozos are not uncommon, nor is passing out at the pool tables or fist-fights spurned by competitive sports on the tube, or even the karaoke lineup. We'll just say it: Barney's is big, dumb, fun.

The Cat Club

8911 Sunset Blvd.
Phone: (310) 657-0888

A nouveau-hesher haven in the heart of the Sunset Strip, The Cat Club, owned by Slim Jim Phantom (the drummer for '80s rockabilly hit-makers Stray Cats) is a litter box of rock star dreams, both broken and burgeoning. Aging long-hairs still grasping their glory days, as well as young upstarts who refuse the pay to play policies that have permeated clubs like the famed Whiskey only stomps away, come here to jam on the cramped room's tiny stage. Unfortunately, the sound system isn't the best, the drinks are notoriously weak and over-priced, and the layout is all wrong for live music viewing. What's right, then? The vampy black and leopard swathed interior and an intangible raunchiness that harkens back to a more decadent time. If you never got a chance to strut the Strip during its hair-metal heyday, this little pit is—after the famed Rainbow—the closest you'll come to conjuring the debauched swagger of that era, especially on Thursdays and Saturdays, when "The Starfuckers" an all-star '70s and '80s rock cover band takes the stage. (The group used to be a hot ticket when the bar first opened, but these days, the players, such as Guns n' Roses' former keyboard player, and guys culled from acts like Slash's Snakepit and Dee Dee Ramone's Band are less recognizable).

The music, whether it be live or not, is usually ear-bleedingly loud (a newish singer/songwriter showcase I've yet to check out might be an exception) and the crowd is rarely boring. Boorish, yes. On weekends at least, you'll see lots of tats, leather and faded concert tees on the guys, and fishnets, cleavage, and dyed/fried hair on the chicks. It might sound like I'm knocking the place a bit, but I actually find it a bracing refuge from some of the Sunset Strip's more upscale rooms. If you get a less than warm reception here, it's not because you're wearing the wrong thing or drove up in the wrong car... it's just 'cause the bar's got a lot of badasses.

(Over) The Rainbow

9015 Sunset Blvd.
Phone: (310) 278-4232

Dive Bar Rating

I know the inclusion of this legendary Sunset Strip landmark won't get me a pot of gold from either dive purists or the place itself, but those who've ever spent any time here, particularly at the bar upstairs—called Over The Rainbow—know why it's here. The bar is not only a dive, it's also a former druggy den. When I interviewed Guns n' Roses' Duff McKagen here a few years ago, he couldn't help but recall the group's wildest, coke-fueled antics upstairs. However, wild times went down in every crevice of the place. In the book, *Straight Whiskey: A Living History of Sex, Drugs and Rock n' Roll*, Poison's Bret Michels recalls the many lascivious times he had in the kitchen!

The establishment as a whole hasn't changed an Aqua-net hardened hair since its heyday. The wood swathed, red booth lined boite is a veritable shrine to the '80s hair metal scene, and I dare you not to turn around and ogle its walls while noshing the large portioned comfort food grub. Distracting shaggy heads abound, leering from nearly every inch of every wall, all pose-y, provocative and cheesetastic. Often, many of these has-beens (and a whole lotta hope-to-bes) will be sitting in the booth next to you, or screeching on a mic upstairs. Still, the Rainbow's illustrious history goes way further back than the metal years. Formerly called The Villa Nova, then owner Vincente Minnelli (Liza's father) was said to have proposed to Judy Garland here, while Marilyn Monroe had her first date (a blind one) with future husband Joe DiMaggio. It has also been reported that John Belushi had his last meal in the kitchen, a bowl of lentil soup, which they've never served since. In the '70s the place was *the* post-gig hangout, a spot where everyone from Led Zeppelin to John Lennon to the King himself, Elvis Presley, would pop in after nights at the nearby Whiskey and Roxy. Much later, the place was immortalized in Guns n' Roses' "November Rain" video.

These days the restaurant and the time-warped mahogany bar above are comparatively tame, hosting karaoke nights, open mics and the like, though the bathrooms recall crazy nights past and often smell of regurgitated pizza (the 'bow's specialty downstairs). The

Rainbow doesn't get the same kind of celeb glow it did back in the day, but I did (and yes, I'm bragging here) do shots with dive aficionado Vince Vaughn upstairs once in the late '90s. For the real raucous Rainbow experience, park it outside on a plastic chair before going upstairs. Christmas lights and clear plastic tarps shelter part of the outdoor bar in its rear area, while the front patio area offers a view of the strip's circus-like action. Here you're likely to see the patios two famous regulars: Cypress Hill's B-Real (often sitting with a crowd and under a—cough, cough—cloud) and Motorhead's Lemmy Killmister. If Lemmy ain't a dive archetype, I don't know who is.

Bars On Film

Blue Room *(Memento)*

Dresden *(Swingers)*

Frolic Room *(Hollywood Confidential)*

HMS Bounty *(Mad Men)*

Fox Fire *(Magnolia)*

Ye Coach & Horses

7617 W Sunset Blvd.
Phone: (323) 876-6900

Located on Sunset Blvd. just before the riotous bumper-to-bumper Strip area, Ye Coach & Horses, which opened back in 1934, lives up to its "ye" prefix with a ramshackle Anglo vibe and plenty of old world personality. As a survivor of the hairspray drenched metal scene that engulfed the area up the street during the '80s, I remember the place as a pick-up joint for struggling rockers (and the pathetic gals willing to support them), but these days it's really not so cruiserville. What hasn't changed is the killer jukebox, impressive beer selection, decent prices (for the area) and cash only status. There's plenty of new drink specials (the Monday Night Social Club offers some good deals, though I like Ladies Night Tuesday, which features $4 shots), and even a music themed one called Tech Noir, an '80s waver.

The room is dark, long and all red and woody, with cobwebbed knick-knacks that look like they may have been there since the times when people actually rode horses. (A drunk dude who guzzled beers next to me one night insisted that, "it used to be dirt roads and pony trails just outside.") However, getting the real historical gist on an oldie like this one (which was a speakeasy at one point) can be difficult, especially when more than one subsequent owner is involved. The bandana sporting bartenders—who are friendly but not exactly knowledgeable about their place of employment—told me that the new owners "aren't very communicative" about the bar. A little net research yields some interesting facts, though, mainly about those who've frequented the English pubber—both Richard Burton and Alfred Hitchcock were allegedly regulars. Quentin Tarantino loves the place, and cited it as one of his favorite things in the City of Angels in an *LA Times* interview. " It's a very *Mean Streets* kind of place," he said. Indeed, the Coach's murky crevices and long-standing struggling musician crowd (the Guitar Center is nearby) make it a good celeb hideout (regulars are said to include James Gandolfini, Christina Applegate, Drew Barrymore and Johnny Knoxville). The bar's Myspace page even has a blog about the star sightings, which would be totally lame if not for this disclaimer: "It is always important to remember that this is not a nightclub, this a bar. Gawking, pestering, or bothering other customers is severely frowned upon by the establishment. Calling the paparazzi is not cute, or even human. Only a mutant would do that."

Eat Here (good, but not free)

Backstage

Chez Jay

The Cork

Dresden

The Rainbow

Red Lion

Ye Rustic Inn

Gay Ol' Times

Akbar

Annex

The Eagle

Le Barcito

Silver Platter

The Spotlight

FAIRFAX DISTRICT

The Kibitz Room

419 N. Fairfax Ave.
Phone: (323) 651-2030

Wise-cracking white-haired waitresses, tatty walls and booths, and a motley assortment of patrons (Jewish families and the Geritol set by day, sleepless party animals in sweat-soaked clubwear by night) make Canter's the dive of delis. But those who really want to get pickled gather not at the bright-lit eating area of this LA institution, but in its darker, dingier adjacent bar, The Kibitz Room. Added to the establishment back in 1961, the bar, like the restaurant, has a transformative quality depending on the time of day. Afternoons, the chatter of elderly locals fills the room, while at night, the volume gets much louder with live bands. The inconsistency of the crowd is reflected in the place's décor. Though Kibitz is very skeezeresque (not much has been changed fixture-wise since the place opened), it's also very rock n' roll. Rock photography shots, the work of the owner's son, Marc Canter, line the walls around the small stage, while articles written about the place (including a piece by yours truly) adorn the walls near the bar. My piece was about the bar's most famous gathering, a Tuesday night jam session featuring local musicians, many of whom went on to stardom: The Wallflowers, The Freewheelers, and The Black Crowes, to name a few. Even, Slash, a friend of the owners son, was known to stop in for some noodling and matzo balls next door.

For me, Kibitz has always had a homey quality, mainly because the Tuesday night gathering was started by a guy I went to Junior High with, keyboard session player Rami Jaffee. I was a regular here during the '90s heyday, and over the years, I got to know both the musicians who hung here as well as the longtime bartender Eric Thatcher (now a booker). I also got to know one of Thatcher's signature concoctions (very, very well), his deceptively delicious and venomously potent, not to mention blush-worthy named pink drink, "The Pussy." Thatcher credits it for his win as "Best Bartender" in *The New Times* newspaper (now folded) back in 2002.

Back during the Tuesday glory days, the crowds were quite young, and sneaking in via the restaurant became a problem, forcing the staff to tighten up their ID-checking policy, which included instituting wristbands for entry and even adding a gate that separated the bar from the deli's adjacent dining room. Though there's still weekly entertainment at the Kibitz including live jazz, rock and pop, the scene is a lot more lax these days. Outside, however, it's a different story. Once a lazy old-world-ish Jew hub, this stretch of Fairfax now has its share of style-conscious stores, and these, coupled with other popular hangs in the area, like the live music room Largo, late night pizza joint Damiano's (my first job!) and another bar, The Dime (which is dark, but not a dive due to its high prices and celeb clientele) have made the area pretty congested at night. Parking is a bitch. If you're down for walking a bit, park three blocks south past Beverly Blvd. at the Farmer's Market, which is a must for nostalgia junkies. Just close your eyes as you walk through the adjacent Grove shopping mall.

The Cinema Bar

CULVER CITY

Backstage Bar & Grill

10400 Culver Blvd.
Phone: (310) 839-3892

Dive Bar Rating

Three words: Culver City Slut. I'm not talking about the looseness of the ladies who happen to reside in this part of Western Los Angeles, but rather, the Backstage's most bodacious and scrumptious cocktail. With ingredients including Stoli Vanilla, Kahlua, Coke and cream, it's tailor-made for gals who like their drinks sweet and are anything but once they've had a few. (Another popular one's called the "Blowjob." Wont even go there.) Which brings me to something the bartender told me the last time I "backed" in: "The bigger the hoop, the bigger the ho." As a gal who often wears the circular ear style, I might have taken offense, but I didn't, since it was said in reference to something that can only be described as "dive bar sculpture." You see, not far from the entrance of this lively liquor haven, a gilded mobile hangs from the ceiling, drooping with gold chains, metallic bangles, rhinestone baubles, and a heaping of hoop earrings, all jewels left behind by babes who've gotten blitzed, bombed and even blacked out on the Slut and the bar's other super-cheap, generously spiked drinks over the past few years. The hoop/ho thing was what some of the staff called the creation in the beginning, but that name thankfully lost its appeal. It's as true as saying all females with lower back tattoos ("tramp stamps") are easy, after all.

Still, there's something about The Backstage, which stands directly across the street from Sony Studios, that seems to bring out the feral side in both sexes. It's divey but nowhere near dangerous, comfortable and roomy but often so packed (especially on karaoke Thursday—Saturday and during Wednesday's house band King Chris and the Groove Thang) that you can't help but meet new people. Other Backstage bonuses: fabulous if super-fattening bar food (garlic fries, mac n' cheese, burgers, wings), an authentic black and white photo booth, multiple screens with multiple sports on non-stop, and ballsy art (pics of icons of eternal cool such as Jimi, Elvis, Clint and Cash, and a poster near the bar that reads "If I want your opinion, I'll beat it out of you"). Don't expect any beatings here, though. It's pretty much happy drunks, locals of all ages and ethnic backgrounds, karaoke fiends talented and terrible, and studio people from the across the street. According to Backstage's website, the space is over seventy years old and the Munchkins from the *Wizard of Oz* called it their (no place like) home away from home.

The Cinema Bar

3967 Sepulveda Blvd.
Phone: (310) 390-1328

Dive Bar Rating

Culver City has enjoyed a notable renaissance over the past several years, boasting both a flourishing art gallery scene and a smattering of trendy new eateries and drinking establishments. Despite this resurgence, the area founded by business mogul Harry H. Culver back in 1913 still retains a lazy simplicity and untouched by time feel in certain spots, particularly along and off of Sepulveda Blvd., where this often shrill shanty stands. Cinema claims the distinction of being the "oldest bar in Culver City" but it's also one of the smallest, and not just in CC, but in all of LA. Which means that when the live music gets going around 10:00 p.m., elbow room is non-existent (the groups themselves take up about a fourth of the room) and conversation virtually impossible. (The tree-lined smoking patio, complete with snack-stocked vending machine, does offer some respite for talky types.) Fortunately, the bands that play here are better than most subpar bar hounds. Mostly of the surf, bluegrass, Americana and jazz variety, there's some real rockin' goin' down in this tiny hole and it's always free. Drinks are equally potent, though probably not as low-priced as one might expect based on the shabby shack surroundings—neon and knick-knacks, a smattering of old tables and chairs, perpetually sticky floors and old movie posters, most noticeably Gottfried Helnwein's *Boulevard of Broken Dreams*, which appropriates Edward Hopper's *Nighthawks* with pop culture icons Humphrey Bogart, Marilyn Monroe and James Dean in the painting's bleak diner setting. Soak up Cinema in the early evening for a sample of its honky tonky heart, when less blaring country and classic rock from the jukebox (George Jones, Johnny Cash, Hank Williams) fills the room and whiskey or gin warms the loins of the hard working (and out of work) local folk. This is the spaghetti western of bars: unfussy, old-timey and more often than not, enhanced by a dramatic soundtrack.

Cozy Inn

11155 Washington Pl.
Phone: (310) 838-3826

Writing about dive bars might seem to be all about fuzzy fun and gregarious good times, but there is an inherent dark side that becomes apparent when you delve deeply. When I paid a visit to the Culver City watering hole known as Cozy, I was in the middle of one of those mercury-in-retrograde kind of weeks, and the thought of sitting in a blackened burrow amongst strangers numbing it with alcohol was quite an appealing prospect. But, this isn't a fade-into-a-corner type of bar, at least not at three in the afternoon, when I chose to cozy up. Not five minutes after parking myself on a stool, I had made friends with two regulars, a sweet fellow named Kermit (whom everyone called the "the frog") and a German chap who was chatty, but not enough to tell me his name. Nursing my $4 cocktail, lovingly made by Cathy (who's been a barmaid here for fourteen years), I was treated to an array of spirited, if silly and slurred arguments, the most intense being about the place's famed shuffleboard game (which takes up a big portion of the room): "The wood has been so lacquered up it may as well be Formica under there!" bit one boozer from a nearby stool. "Tom's right," agreed our German pal. "They haven't respected de vood [wood]." "It's still a nice board," countered Kermit the friendly frogman, whom I ended up bonding with and eventually, talking to pretty intently. Kermit, as it turned out, was dealing with some personal stuff too, and as we chatted tearily and maybe too revealingly, I was reminded that the main allure of drinking establishments, especially the divey ones, is the camaraderie and comfort that can be found in them.

While the cliché about bartenders being pseudo-therapists is sometimes accurate, at neighborhood dives like Cozy, the environment can be more like group therapy—with lots of liquid medication. Let me introduce you to rest of the group then: there's Nigel, a flamboyant fellow who hangs here every morning and whose bleached head adorns the joint in two eye-catching 8x10s above the otherwise non-script wood paneled bar (Processions of photos, most of which feature regular Cozy patrons with some kind of fish they caught, line the entire bar). Another luggish regular by the name of Kenny was not only leering from above as well, catch in hand, but also near the opposite wall via four prominently placed caricature drawings—the kind artists do on the street—from one of his vacations in Cabo. He'll tell ya all about it when you come in. And if by chance he's not there, I promise you that one of the above will be. Cozy is its crowd, but if you're not the social type, you might want to go elsewhere. There are some non-human amusements, though: the aforementioned shuffleboard, the pool tables (which seem to get some real shark action, with many bringing their own cues), the rednecky jukester, the dismal bathrooms featuring cheap powdered public school soap (it exfoliates!), and Cozy's sneaky rear exit to its parking lot. This one seems made for quick escape: from the law, the ol' lady/man, and maybe more than anything else, the tough truths that hard liquor and conversing with strangers can reveal.

Joxer's Daly

11168 Washington Blvd.
(310) 838-3745

Joxer's Daly might be more of a blue-collar pub than a dive, but it's got a gruffness about it that makes it a fave with hardcore sports junkies, hooch lovin' expats, and Culver City curmudgeons alike. And though things get mighty loud and raucous in this spacious, forty year-old bar and grill (especially during big sporting events: Celtics for soccer and Redskins for football rule here) it never gets too unruly, probably because of the room's other regulars; it's also a popular cop and firefighter hangout. While most of them hang here off-duty in plain clothes, Daly's décor indicates its affection for the men in uniform, as wall accents and accoutrements include the front end of a CHP bike protruding from the main front wall, a life-size statue of a firefighter, and a wall devoted to 9/11 (by total coincidence, my first foray into the place happened to be on the anniversary of that tragic day, and the bar was giving a portion of the proceeds to the families of the firefighters who perished in the Twin Towers). Law enforcement patches create a garland-like affect behind the bar, along with newspaper clippings and hand-written notes and signs, the most prominent of the latter being that week's "Big Loser" of the Tuesday night money giveaway. If you sign up to win the weekly $100 prize and aren't there to pick it up that night, your name is posted everywhere for the regulars to mock.

With its sport heavy focus, gun-toting crowd, greasy but good food selection (the fish and chips rock) and foxy jeaned barmaids, Joxer's is definitely a testosterone-drenched joint, but there's also something here for gals, and not just the ones looking for a man. The little girls room is pimped out like no other. The closet-size room itself isn't much to look at, but the toiletry selection is unreal: makeup, hair scrunchies, mints, "feminine deodorant sprays," all the stuff the fancy clubs with bathroom attendants boast and then some, all free for the taking. Entertainment is offered weekly (karaoke, bad bar bands) and actual athletes have been known to pop in (during his first LA Galaxy season, David Beckham came in once and left the waitress a $900 tip on a $100 tab!). If that and those sprays can't bring in the ladies, nothing will. Still, it's primarily a guy's clubhouse. A prominent sign (they like signs here) next to the telephone behind the bar lets the fellas know the bar's got their back if the wifey should call. It reads: *$1: not here, $2: on his way out, $3: just left, $4: haven't seen him all day, $5: who?*

They Will Rock You (Live Music)

The Dresden

The Cat Club

Kibitz Room

La Cita

Redwood Bar

Relax

Silverlake Lounge

Scarlet Lady Saloon

5411 Sepulveda Blvd
Phone: (310) 391-9079

Dive Bar Rating

Much has been made of the rivalry between The Scarlet Lady Saloon and The Tattletale Lounge two spaces down, but according to Red, the Lady's sweet, ginger braid-sporting bartender, it's all a lot of hogwash. Everyone gets along on the strip, he insists, and whether or not that's in fact true, it is the case inside this place. "Hi Red…Bye Red!" I hear over a dozen times as I nurse my $5 tumbler at the bar. "Hi Blanche…Bye Pam!" he replies back each and every time. (Yes, in a bar like this, the gals have names like Blanche.) With no less than six TV screens broadcasting every game any buff could possibly want and a noticeable female contingent (though they're pretty much all seasoned broads…I was the youngest filly in the place on my visits), Scarlet is anything but the scary house of horrors it's sometimes portrayed to be. Driving by, it does look a little ominous, especially with the ubiquitous sullied smoker crews who hang outside under the jazzy, snazzy old sign. Not content to stand, this scruffy assortment of oddballs literally have chairs that they prop right in front of the bar, old man on the porch style. Walking past them to enter can make a gal feel a bit vulnerable. But once inside, it's obvious that The Lady is nothing but a chill n' cheap working man—and woman's—sanctum; ho-hum and harmless, especially during weekday happy hour. Things gets a lot livelier at night, especially with a busy schedule that offers blues bands and burlesque (Wednesday), beer pong (Thursday), Karaoke (Friday and Saturday) and Pub Quiz (Sunday). Expect more back and forth with The Tale after dark, not to mention more self-proclaimed cougars and tail chasing tigers on the prowl.

Tattle Tale

5401 Sepulveda Blvd.
Phone: (310) 390-2489

Local yokels, inebriated expats and overflow from The Scarlet Lady next door make for a sloshed n' sundry mix at Tattle Tale, which touts itself as the "#1 Dive Bar" on its business cards and rubber foam beer can cozies, which also happen to feature the bar's sexy mascot, a pin-up style gal dressed in what looks like a kitty cat costume (Though it has a more suggestive name, the 'Lady next door lacks any sexy imagery on its marketing materials). According to the cozy, "Roger's Exciting Tattle Tale Room" (the bar's full name) is forty-five years old; however, the place doesn't exactly live up to its titillating moniker or mascot these days. Small, dank, and definitely more of a dude bar than its neighbor, TT is real and friendly, no matter how rough some of the regulars may be. It does get rowdy during the nightly scaryoke sessions, which take on a comic croon-a-thon feel when the regulars get in on the action. Muffin-top jeaned mamas tackling Madonna, wobbly rednecks channeling Tom Jones and the occasional serious, kick-ass crooner (notably the female bartenders) make for an *American Idol* on acid spectacle. Both The Scarlet and Tattle Tale have cool old signs, and if there was a competition in that department, I'd give the nod to Tattle's red and blue optical eye-fuck. Are the red beams behind its lettering straight or slanted? The answer often varies with how many drinks you've downed.

MAR VISTA

Lost & Found

11700 National Blvd.
Phone: (310) 397-7772

Drowning away the day, quietly glued to the tube with a handful of the hard stuff is why older gents come to this smoky Mar Vista mini-mall spot. However, after 5:00 or so, a noisier—if still leisurely—atmosphere takes over. You see, when men of a certain age hang out for hours at a bar, they tend to get quite loquacious, and if you're a young lady (and by young I mean under fifty), you will be treated to classic, amplified-for-your-benefit sound bites from the drunken gent set. "I carry a picture of my wife with me when I come to this bar," proclaims one graying chap. "When she starts looking good, I know it's time to go home." It only gets more obnoxiously amusing from there, as grandpa's hefty sidekick, who announces that's he's recently divorced, chimes in with the wifey cracks. "You know how to cure an oversexed Jewish woman? Marry her!" Even the seemingly mild-mannered bartender has something to say: "You know what's the best birth control? Wedding Cake." Everyone in the place chuckles, even the solo drunks who don't appear to even like the noisy cluster of these would-be comedians. These joke-filled, jolly moments are entertaining, yes, but there's a somber side to the lovelorn laughs, as men who spend all day in a bar generally do have problems—or no one—at home. Which is why they keep coming back, of course. Well, insanely cheap drinks might have something to do with it too: $3.50 for vodka cranberries, Greyhounds and Manhattans (Absolut in 'em will run ya $4). There is no top shelf booze in sight, but what is: décor that hasn't been altered since the place opened in 1974, a beaten billiards table, a birthday board behind the bar (with names like "Dottie"), a cute kids-room-appropriate puppy poster that reads "Lost and Found," free popcorn and a smoking area near the back door (not quite outside of it) that definitely contributes to the front room's fusty, yet strangely comforting stench.

SANTA MONICA

Chez Jay

1657 Ocean Ave.
Phone: (310) 395-1741

This shabby oceanside bistro and bar has long been a self-proclaimed "celebrity dive," which might sound paradoxical, but actually makes sense once you sail in and see its sawdust and peanut shell-covered floors, checkered table-cloths, the giant mounted tuna over the bar and the various seafaring ephemera. The place is cozy and dark and pretty much unchanged since Jay Fiondella opened its doors in 1959. Back then, Fiondella (who passed in 2008) was somewhat of a thespian, and he made the bar into a haven for old Hollywood, drawing stars with tasty seafood and steaks, very, very stiff drinks and most importantly, privacy (he would often kick out camera-toting fans). Jay's was a fave of The Rat Pack, especially ol' blue eyes himself, and John F. Kennedy and his alleged side dish Ms. Marilyn Monroe are said to have had more than one romantic rendezvous here. Henry Kissinger came by so often they named a backroom table after him, and Astronaut Alan Shepard even took one of the bar's famed peanuts to the moon, later presenting the place with a signed affidavit that the nut had indeed traveled in space with him. (The framed document still hangs to the left of the bar.)

Jay's is like a sweet little seashell that's managed to stay afloat in the abyss of upscale hotels and restaurants in the area, and while it might not be the fame magnet it once was, it still gets cited by celebs as an old school fave. Sean Penn held his birthday party in the backroom a few years ago, which the co-owner Michael Anderson calls the "VIP room." Anderson will be there most nights to seat you, tell you the history of the place (and hurry you up from one of the coveted booths if there's a line out front). The food is okay and the drinks average priced, but it's the nostalgia-soaked nautical nest itself that's the main draw. Jay may be gone but his memories (and some salacious secrets) will apparently be revealed in a book about the bar he penned before his death with writer Jon Stebbins. Via Stebbins website, an excerpt from the book *It Happened At Chez Jay's* reveals that a real incident there inspired Warren Beatty's memorable under the table oral-sex scene in *Shampoo*, as well as the infamous leak of the Pentagon Papers to the press, both occurred at table number 10. I'm guessing Jay's potent pours played a role in each.

The Daily Pint

2310 Pico Blvd.
Phone: (310) 450-7631

The selection at the Daily Pint is so amazing that you might say it couldn't possibly be labeled a dive. But to me, Daily's diviness is only enhanced by its copious collection of brews and stews. For one thing, it appears they don't have enough room in the back of the place for all their poisons, namely the drafty stuff, as kegs literally adorn every crevice of the two-roomed pub (under shelving, near the pool table and shuffleboard games, under tables) and what looks like about a thousand bottles—some in un-labeled moonshiney-looking jugs—gleam from behind and above the bar. A giant chalkboard across from the main ordering area boasts the latest offerings, debuts and limited time specials, and with over 150 regularly stocked bottled beers, a total of 33 taps, plus 3 beer engines serving cask conditioned ales, not to mention special events like scotch tastings, beer debut bashes and limited edition sampling soirees, this is a place for serious drinkers. The mood here is anything but, though, and on weekends it gets downright zoo-like, with the bartenders scrambling to serve the mix of millennial yuppie dudes and beach-bum-cum-hipsters ("vintage" rock t-shirts and sun-streaked hair) of all ages. There's a huge screen broadcasting whatever the night's biggest game happens to be, but most are pre-occupied by the billiards and shuffleboard tables in the game-packed side of the bar, which also gets rowdier, hence grubbier. A guy spilled his pilsner on me during my last visit and seemed to feel worse about losing some of his precious nectar than soaking my shirt. And, nobody cleaned up the puddle below us. Dust-bunnies hang from the ceiling, and the walls could use a scrub, but you get the feeling the owners here aren't out to impress anybody with the bar itself (the "n" in Pint on the sign out front fell off and stayed off for a long time til a recent repair). They let their menu do it for them.

Gaslite

2030 Wilshire Blvd.
Phone: (310) 829-2382

Dive Bar Rating

🍾

Karaoke bars always feature one or more of the following archetypes: semi-pros looking for free rehearsal time; the shy, seemingly meek type who turns, Incredible Hulk-like, into a (not bad) belter after a few drinks; the shrill-voiced freak who seems to get off on torturing everyone in the place with his/her shiteous shrieks; and the clueless crooner who sucks balls but actually thinks he or she sounds good (this sad breed is what makes watching *American Idol's* audition segments so trainwreckishly entertaining). At the Gaslite, you'll see all of these 'okesters, especially the latter two. Not that it matters how good anybody is, really, as crowd sing-alongs are common, and people here often get so lit and loud that the person who happens to be standing on the tiny stage in the back of the place is often inconsequential.

On weekends—when there's almost always a line outside to get in—those who sign-up for the singer's spotlight usually have to share it. Drunk dudes you don't know jump up on the mic to fill in choruses, the karaoke MC makes obtusely humorous comments, and if you happen to be here around midnight, the dance floor becomes a hedonist hump-a-thon with guys and gals grinding and bumping and even falling all over each other, particularly in between song selections when they play bits of club banger hits. It's hilarious to observe the shift from shake-fest to communal choir that takes place. Examples: Two very tan blondes sing "Drops of Jupiter," then the DJ plays Kanye West's "Gold Digger" and everyone bounces. A nerdy guy wearing a CBGB t-shirt croons "Sweet Caroline" (with the crowd filling in the "oh, oh, oh" after each chorus at the top of their lungs), then the DJ spins Missy Elliot's "Work It" and butts start bouncin.' This disjointed debauchery actually works, mainly because the establishment is so trodden and frat house-like, from its less than reliable soundsystem and mics to its dirty brown carpets, mirrored walls and ill placed oil paintings. No kegs, but they do have a "bucket of beers" for $12, a popcorn machine, multiple TVs with all the games on and a huge bouncer at the door for those times when the choral carousing causes a clash. And I'm not talking about bad versions of "Rock the Casbah."

The Joker

2827 Pico Blvd.
Phone: (310) 264-9856

Dive Bar Rating

With a name like The Joker, one might expect a wild atmosphere, but this old Santa Monica sipper, while chock full of accoutrements and amusements (old video games, a futurist jukebox, pool tables, wall-to-wall wood paneling, year-round Christmas lights, pics of clowns and, of course, Batman's nemesis) still has a fairly unremarkable, blah feel. Which may be why so many people tend to recall famous bar scenes from movies when they refer to the place. It's been likened to one of the blood bathed-dives in *Carlitos Way* and the pal who first took me there told me that she and her girlfriends called it, "The bar from *The Accused*." Yikes. They said it jokingly, but I wore a loose sweatshirt just in case my first time in. It was not necessary.

Aside from an eerie 3D picture of Heath Ledger from *Dark Knight* on prime display, this place is anything but scary. You might find wanna-be gangster/grease-monkey types playing pool, a mullet, or a trucker cap or two, and definitely an old timer contingent lingering on the rickety stools or in the adjacent pool room, but the vibe is more dull than dangerous, even with the thunderous sludge of heavy metal and classic rock on the 'box. The kindly white-haired codger manning the bar is amicable enough, though he does seem annoyed, and apparently always is, when newbies come in unaware that they only take cash. He defrosts pretty quickly for us ladies, thankfully. If you start feeling literary, there's a little bookshelf full of tattered paperbacks for your perusal, right next to a microwave for warming up a Swanson TV dinner, your lunch from Micky D's or leftovers from nearby Rae's, the coolest old fashioned diner in Santa Monica and maybe all of LA I suggest you bring in the greasiest grub you can, 'cause with drinks this cheap (wells averaging $4-$5), going overboard is easy. Soaking up the sauce before even attempting to survive the scrutiny of Santa Monica's overzealous police patrollers is a must.

Speakeasy

1326 Pico Blvd.
Phone: (310) 450-4989

To be a regular at Speakeasy, you've really gotta be a fan of drab slabs. One of the plainest, dreariest, weirdest dives atmosphere-wise on the Westside, this bar's exterior suggests a strip club, with something loud, flashy and illicit going on inside. Which makes it all the more shocking once you walk in. The place is so laid back it's in slow motion, and the most exciting visual element is a tacky gold-lace/marbleized mirror behind the bar area (the kind one might see in a '70s bathroom). It all serves as the perfect backdrop for the servers: Scottish ladies in mom jeans reeking of stogies, Aqua-net and cheap perfume. They aren't very friendly at first (heard they usually favor the gents over the ladies), but they do warm up eventually and are surprisingly skilled at cocktail concoction; mixed drinks are tongue tingling and cheap. Special props for the Bloody Marys, which are hearty and perfectly spiced. Though there seems to be a good selection of booze, identical bottles of cheap Gallo style wine adorn a whole shelf behind the bar. Odd. Even odder: the crowd. Think Harmony Korine's *Gummo* (and not in the cool Chloe Sevigny way) singing karaoke in pitches so bad, they're actually brilliant. This is one of those spots you "take over" for the novelty of it, which is easy to do, as around 11 p.m. on a Saturday night, there's about ten people in the rather spacious room, and five of them are here for a birthday party. At about the time "Rocket Man" emanates from under the brightly lit pool table area, and the b-day boy gets on the mic to sing it with a snazzy cadence that may or may not be inspired by William Shatner, my drink kicks in and I start to see the appeal of this very strange rabbit hole. You never know what you might find inside, and even when it's empty, there's something to wonder about.

More Diving by the Beach:

Roosterfish 1302 Abbot Kinney Blvd. Venice. Phone: (310) 392-2123
Hinanos 15 Washington Blvd. Venice. Phone: (310) 822-3902
Prince O' Whales 335 Culver Blvd. Playa Del Rey. Phone: (310) 823-9826

INGLEWOOD, MID-CITY

The Annex

835 S La Brea Ave.
Phone: (310) 671-7323

Depending on when you enter this notoriously grimy Inglewood gay bar, you'll find either a packed house of bodacious bootie-bumping black men (Monday, and Friday-Saturday when DJs spin hip-hop and club hits), or a nearly empty bar with an elderly Redd Foxx looking gentleman belting out Mariah Carey with the jukebox and a trio of tipsy trannies gazing at him admiringly. I got the latter when I stopped by, and was grateful for it. Like many bars that get clubby on certain nights, Annex's charms can be somewhat masked by the mayhem that accompanies the music and lights. When it's just the regulars, however, you get the essence of the place. At Annex, that essence is drinks so strong—if not exactly cheap at $7—that I have to ask (twice) for my Jack and Coke to be weakened with more soda; friendly bartenders who don't seem one bit phased by the fact that you're an obvious outsider (not gay, not black, not hammered to the point of incoherence); and of course, characters like the Carey crooner, who later treats the half empty room to heartfelt renditions of Toni Braxton, Mary J Blige and Chaka... Chaka Khan.

The place has been around for thirty years under the same owner, and is painted a calming mint green, with black booths and mirrored walls. The bathrooms are more chaotic. Pepto pink walls and signs everywhere that warn against males entering and smoking ("or you will be asked to leave!") suggest some serious shenanigans have taken place here, especially inside the stalls, which have had their individual doors removed. You pee for all to see, which I discovered after walking in on a masculine looking, dread-locked gal doing her business. "The drag queens fucked it up for the rest of us, child!" she says as she quickly wipes and runs. Kinda thought she might be a queen—or king?—herself. Obviously, the thrones here have seen lots of both, a royal flush as it were. I opt to hold it.

The Beacon

950 W Manchester Blvd.
Phone: (310) 649-4011

Dive Bar Rating

Rant time. A lot of people who pride themselves as hardcore dive bar heads are haters. They hate the vapid vampiness of the club scene (understandable). They hate the high price of going out (ditto). But less tolerable—and I know you're not one of these—they abhor and disparage entire neighborhoods (Silver Lake and Echo Park for being too hip, West Hollywood and Beverly Hills for being too fake). They make broad statements about establishments in these areas via blogs and websites like Yelp, essentially slagging their popularity because they don't like the haircuts they see there. What I've discovered on my dive bar adventures, though, is that many of these same people who think their definition of "dive" is the end all and be all don't actually dig that deep when they go out to drink. They don't leave their comfort zones, even if they act like they do. Old people bars are one thing, but you won't find these types in the ghetto where they might be the only white person for miles (same goes for people of color in white trashy taverns). They don't want to be the straight (sore) thumb in the gay bar full of flaming femmes and butchy bears either. And the ladies? Who doesn't dread being the fresh meat on display in an unfamiliar wolves den? I'll admit that I've had fleeting feelings of this sort while bar-hopping, but ultimately, I learned from these experiences and opened my mind, both about myself and my city. (I hope you have reading this as well). End of rant.

By the time I stepped foot into the Beacon, near the end of my juiced-up journeys, my perspective had evolved. The circular shaped, multi-window and wood-paneled room is—like The Annex—in Inglewood, a predominantly African-American region of Los Angeles, and other than the bartender (a hippie-looking dude with a greasy, grey ponytail) and the friend he rambled on with all night, my husband and I were the only white folk there on a weeknight. But with the possible exception of my variant song choices on the digital jukebox (The Stones and Al Green vs. everyone else's endless Lil Wayne selections), nobody cared. And that's what makes a good dive: it is a place to drink away in an environment that's not focused on race, class, interests… or hairstyles. The Beacon, open since the '50's, has all the aforementioned qualities of a good dive: low-prices ($4-$5), two pool tables, several TVs (not flatscreens but the big clunky ones), and the already mentioned jukebox. One more plus: it's across the street from the LAX Firing Range, so if you do happen to be one of the hostile types I mentioned above, you can get out your aggressions on a paper target.

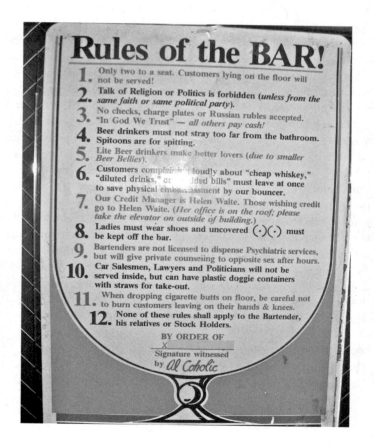

Rules of the BAR!

1. Only two to a seat. Customers lying on the floor will not be served!

2. Talk of Religion or Politics is forbidden (*unless from the same faith or same political party*).

3. No checks, charge plates or Russian rubles accepted. "In God We Trust" — *all others pay cash!*

4. Beer drinkers must not stray too far from the bathroom. Spitoons are for spitting.

5. Lite Beer drinkers make better lovers (*due to smaller Beer Bellies*).

6. Customers complaining loudly about "cheap whiskey," "diluted drinks," or padded bills" must leave at once to save physical embarrassment by our bouncer.

7. Our Credit Manager is Helen Waite. Those wishing credit go to Helen Waite. (*Her office is on the roof; please take the elevator on outside of building.*)

8. Ladies must wear shoes and uncovered $(\cdot)(\cdot)$ must be kept off the bar.

9. Bartenders are not licensed to dispense Psychiatric services, but will give private counseiing to opposite sex after hours.

10. Car Salesmen, Lawyers and Politicians will not be served inside, but can have plastic doggie containers with straws for take-out.

11. When dropping cigarette butts on floor, be careful not to burn customers leaving on their hands & knees.

12. None of these rules shall apply to the Bartender, his relatives or Stock Holders.

BY ORDER OF

X

Signature witnessed

by *Al Coholic*

The Cork

4771 W Adams Blvd.
Phone: (323) 731-2030

Dive Bar Rating

Don't let the diligent pat down (dudes) or request to peek inside your purse (ladies) by the large, possibly-packing security guard at the door deter you from going to The Cork, as it happens to be one of the warmest, friendliest eating and drinking spots in this part of town, with residents from surrounding areas as diverse as Inglewood, Baldwin Hills and Compton convening for superior grub and treacherously mixed drinks. Neither are cheap, but they are worth the seemingly high-ish prices ($8-$10 range for cocktails, $10-$16 range for food). The barmaids and the kitchen cook's don't seem to know the word "moderation" and even the frou-frou drinks are high-octane (you will crash and burn on the Cadillac Margarita). Despite what its name might suggest, the place doesn't have a very extensive wine list, and some choices don't have corks at all, but small bottles that screw off. But you don't come to The Cork if you're a vino connoisseur any more than you come here to dig in the scene with a gangsta lean. It's generally an older urban middle class crowd with all types mixed in. Though a banner inside boasts it's been around for forty-four years, the antique arrow sign out front seems all that remains of the original appearance. It's pretty clean and modern inside these days, though kitschy touches like a clock that looks like a giant watch provide some off-kilter flavor. The best thing about this one? A very palpable female energy (the waitresses, barmaids and cooks are mostly young-ish females and their back and forth chatter and groovin' to the juke—which favors nu-soul like Sade, Soul2Soul and Maxwell, over hip-hop—makes for a nice, relaxed feel). Love the sign behind the bar that reads, "Drink til he's cute," a sassy spin on the perpetually sexist bar signs that grace most dives.

More Diving Nearby:

The Office 206 E Grand Ave. El Segundo Phone: (310) 648-3131
The Greatest 13700 Inglewood Ave. Hawthorne Phone: (310) 973-9241

I adhered to a twenty minute rule for my dive write-ups: if the bar took longer than twenty minutes to get to from downtown, it didn't qualify. However, Long Beach—on the edge of Los Angeles County just before Orange County—deserves dive note for the following:

Flite Room 4111 Lakewood Blvd. Lakewood Phone: (562) 425-5559

The Hawaiian Room 9875 Alondra Blvd. Bellflower Phone: (562) 866-9252

The Hideaway 5523 South St. Lakewood 90713 Phone: (562) 867-3187

Poor Richards 6412 E Stearns St. Long Beach Phone: (562) 596-0882

Thirsty Isle 4317 E Carson St. Long Beach Phone: (562) 421-3571

Sweet Water Saloon 1201 E Broadway Long Beach Phone: (562) 432-7044

Nana's Cocktails 329 W Willow St. Long Beach Phone: (562) 595-7926

The 10 Best of the Best
(cheap drinks, cool staff, intangible bar bliss)

1. Frolic Room

2. Fox Fire Room

3. Backstage Bar

4. Burgundy Room

5. Kibitz Room

6. Colorado Bar

7. Frank N Hanks

8. The Short Stop

9. Chez Jay

10. Rustic Inn

RIP (Rest In Puke) - The Best Dead Dives

The Blacklight

Tiny's

The Red Garter

Sarna's

The Dume Room

The Bitter Redhead

The Now Voyager

Rae's Lounge

Ski Room

Zatar's

The Shamrock

Al's Bar

Jukebox Heroes?

A note about Jukes. A tally of the best ones would have been an important list about five years ago, but the advent of digital jukeboxes—which you'll find in even the most sordid of bars these days—has pretty much obliterated the divide between good and bad. The pros are obvious: patrons can download an endless selection of music from any genre, from obscurities to pop hits. The cons? Individual bars don't really craft the musical scheme of their rooms anymore, and as anyone who has ever been in their favorite rock hole when an outsider's thrown on Britney Spears knows, the digital jukes can be a real mood killer. Some bars are still holding out with CD-selector boxes, and most of these are noted in their individual write-ups.

Index